About the Author

Carol Lynne Steingreaber graduated in 1987 from Loras College in Dubuque, Iowa with double majors in English Literature and Writing, proclaiming on her graduation day, "Someday I will write a book!"

She worked as a correspondent, proofreader and copywriter in Des Moines, Iowa for six years before starting her tenure as a stay-at-home mom.

Exhausted from answering the question, "What do you do all day?" (Here's another unconventional tip: never ask a stay-at-home mom or dad this question unless you want to get cold-cocked), she took a position as a marketing director in 2006. In 2013, Carol started writing her first humorous autobiography, *Pants Optional*, in her free time.

She currently resides in Cedar Rapids, Iowa with her husband, Paul.

Dedication

Loras Duhawk 1986,

Your unwavering support from the moment I wrote my first sentence has touched my heart in ways you can never imagine. Thanks for encouraging me to share with the world some of the fun we've had. Lastly, thanks for racing me back in October of 1983. Pretty sure that was the moment I fell in love.
~ Loras Duchick 1987

Kate and Nick,

This book is for you. Laugh. Enjoy. Remember. Be thankful. And for heaven's sake pass along UNconventional Tip #15 to your kids. I'm counting on it.
~ All my love, Mom

Carol L. Steingreaber

PANTS OPTIONAL

AUSTIN MACAULEY
PUBLISHERS LTD.

A CIP catalogue record for this title is available from the British Library.

Most of this book was written from direct experience but all from memory, with a few stories told to author from elderly parents and siblings. Thank you for allowing for any minor memory inaccuracies or exaggerations.

Book Cover Design by Mary P. Donahue

ISBN 978 1 78554 733 1 (Paperback)
ISBN 978 1 78554 734 8 (Hardback)
ISBN 978 1 78554 735 5 (E-Book)

www.austinmacauley.com

First Published (2016)
Austin Macauley Publishers Ltd.
25 Canada Square
Canary Wharf
London
E14 5LQ

Acknowledgments

Thank you to all the women who took time out of their busy lives to read my drafts: Cathy, Brenda, Stephanie, Patti, Sarah, Ann, Joyce, Kourtné, Mary, Kelly and Jane. Your enthusiasm, comments and encouragement will never be forgotten.

Mary P. Donahue, working with you on my book cover has been a joy and an honor. You are a talented and amazing woman.

Contents

A man's got to take a lot of punishment to write a really funny book.

~ Ernest Hemingway

People with a sense of humor tend to be less egocentric and more realistic in their view of the world and more humble in moments of success and less defeated in times of travail.

~ Bob Newhart

UNconventional Tip #1

A Sense Of Humor Is Not Optional

When you look like this growing up you learn three things:

1) Have a sense of humor.
2) Don't let your sister (who is NOT a beautician) cut your hair.
3) Run fast so the bullies can't catch you.

I was everything you shouldn't be in a family of seven: quiet, shy, naïve, humble, unassuming, kind and trusting. Little did I know all of these qualities would later be used against me by my brothers and sisters. Thank God I was the baby of the family. It allotted me certain privileges, but those were short-lived when my third sister came along seven years after me. Once Brenda arrived I lost my lofty throne and was immediately thrown into the mix, trying to make my way as a middle child.

I grew up in Iowa, sixth of seven siblings. Add two loud parents and put us in an eight hundred square foot house. It was a sitcom that couldn't be turned off after thirty minutes. My life made for some moments that required a sense of humor. Let's be honest, my whole life has required a sense of humor (cue picture from previous page). I quickly learned I was amassing a whole arsenal of unconventional tips I could use to help others with their journey on the road through life and motherhood. I just had to get through mine first. Alive. Sane. Wiser. And hopefully wearing pants.

It all started with Mom and Dad. They had two things going for them: they could find the humor in anything and a 5 o'clock Saturday night Catholic Mass anywhere in the continental United States. My older siblings would argue with my parents, trying to convince them there was such a thing as "travel dispensation" when on vacation. My parents would laugh and proceed to drive us miles and miles out of our way to attend a Saturday night mass. I didn't mind as the church was always a lot nicer and dryer then any campground we were driving to. Here they are on their wedding day, October 22, 1955.

TV blaring. Doors slamming. Someone hollering. Shower running. Toilet flushing. Someone laughing. Phone ringing. Pots and pans clanging. Dog barking. Someone crying. Our house was never quiet. Due to that fun fact, we had the added bonus of my parents yelling most of the time because they didn't want us saying, "I didn't hear you tell me to take out the garbage, clean the kitchen or vacuum the basement."

Raising two kids shy of a baseball team afforded my parents the privilege of saying exactly what was on their minds, leaving nothing open to interpretation. There was no time to spare as they blurted out orders knowing they would be interrupted at any moment.

Looking back, they taught me four things that stuck. To be specific, I'm sure they taught me more than four, but these were the ones I heard when I wasn't hiding from them to avoid more chores.

Have a sense of humor.

Marry someone who makes you laugh.

No topic is ever off the table.

Don't take life so seriously.

My parents laugh a lot. They are always saying, "A sense of humor is one thing in life that's free!" We grew up watching Johnny Carson, Carol Burnett and Lucy, Hogan's Heroes, Mash, Bob Newhart, Doris Day, Dick Van Dyke and Ozzie and Harriet. With all of this comedy constantly playing on TV, it's only natural that some rubbed off on me and my family. We all think we're funny. *Think* being the key word.

My parents will tell you that without a sense of humor they never would have made it 56 years. Period. So marry someone who makes you laugh.

When I was in college, my parents, Colleen and Jerry, met Paul for the first time (then boyfriend – kind of fiancé – since he had given me a "promise ring" with a diamond the size of a grain of sand). You would think I would hear comments like "He seems nice. He has good teeth. Is he Catholic? What's this 'golf' that he speaks of?"

Naturally, after our day together, I was dying to hear their thoughts.

Me: "Well, Mom and Dad, what did you think of Paul?"

My parents fold their arms and get all concerned. Neither speaks (so unlike them). Finally Mom starts to comment, with Dad nodding in agreement.

Mom: "Um…honey. We don't know how to tell you this but…Jerry, you tell her."

I look at my dad.

Dad: "Honey, what we are trying to say is…I don't know how to break this to you but…Paul isn't funny. He didn't say one funny thing all day."

Me: "Um…okay I didn't see that coming. Paul would have said something funny if you hadn't interrupted him a million times while he was trying to converse with you."

Actually, their comments did not surprise me because I have learned not to be shocked by anything that comes out of my parents' mouths. Hence, the third non-negotiable item: no topic is ever off the table.

Paul and I were home from college one weekend – yes we were still dating – and took a nap together in the middle bedroom, door open of course. I was still following the rules from my youth: no boys in the bedroom unless the door remains open.

After our nap my dad cornered Paul.

Dad (all serious): "Paul, I want to sit down and talk to you about something important."

Paul: "Okay Jerry."

Dad: "Now I know you and Carol aren't having sex before you get married because that is how we raised her. However, I hate to see you taking a nap with her because you are going to develop a case of something called 'Blue Balls'."

Paul: Stunned silence with mouth gaping open.

Dad: "Now, this is a real thing and can be very painful. Once you are married you will never have it again because you are able to have sex. But napping together can bring it on so I just want to help you avoid 'Blue Balls' as best I can until you are married." My dad is now standing, acting like he just delivered a public service announcement and shaking Paul's hand and clapping him on the back.

Dad: "You're welcome, Son."

My dad leaves the kitchen and walks downstairs to watch football on TV.

Paul remains standing motionless in kitchen trying to figure out what just happened, why he feels icky, if he really wants to marry into my family and feeling very relieved it was just a promise ring he gave me.

Their last words of wisdom, don't take life so seriously, is the one piece of their advice I took very seriously. And thank God I did. It got me through the blue balls moment and many others on my road through life and motherhood.

UNconventional Tip #2

Have Your Favorites

The only thing all of my siblings (not parents) have ever agreed on is that we all love my sister, Brenda, the best. Brenda is the baby of the family. She really was a surprise to my parents. I remember Mom sitting on the bathroom toilet crying. She never closed the door when she used the bathroom. None of us did. There was only one bathroom for many years in our house and we weren't allowed to lock the door in case someone needed to pee more than you needed to brush your teeth or pop a zit in the mirror.

Me: "Mom, why are you crying?"

Mom: "I'm going to have another baby. I'm too old for this."

Mom was 35 when she found out she was going to have Brenda. Not old for this day and age, but back in the early 70's she seemed to think it was. This unborn child was about to usurp my role as the baby of the family. I was only seven, but I already knew that this was as close to being a queen as I was ever going to get. I was treated like royalty by my siblings. If my dad was running the odd errand he would ask *just* me if I wanted to tag along and he'd always buy me a treat. That was all about to change in a few short months.

Once Brenda was born I was completely forgotten about by my parents and siblings. Don't be sad for me. Occasionally this actually worked in my favor. My name would be the last off my mom's lips when she wanted me to do a certain chore. (If you have ever been around parents with lots of kids, you'll know that when they are trying to call a certain child and they can't think of their name they go through this whole litany of their kids' names until they get to the one they want. My mom would do that all the time.) This is how it worked; when she'd needed a chore done the first name on her lips would always be Brenda, the baby, but of course she was too little to help so then Mom would start at the top of the batting order and yell for Theresa, Rick, Sherri, Marty, David and if none of them answered to step up to the plate, I would hear, "Carol?". Or to be more specific "Whoever you are, please fold the clothes in the dryer."

It was easy to disappear in my family. I was a very quiet child. I could sit and play dolls by myself for hours. People would trip over me and say, "Oh, I didn't see you there." I would observe and listen and avoid drawing attention to myself. I used to pretend I was invisible. It wasn't hard. Once, when my brothers were supposed to be babysitting me, I leashed up Kipper, our black poodle, and walked a half mile to the Hy-Vee store. I was five. I walked in with Kipper, grabbed a handful of candy from a checkout line where no one was checking out and left the store. No one saw me. No one followed me out or came after me. My parents eventually found me behind some apartments sitting under a shade tree with candy wrappers all around and Kipper curled up next to me. I mean, come on, after that incident how could I **not** believe I was invisible?

Plus, my siblings did not want me to get too much attention. If ever I did, they would tease me and say, "You're just getting special attention because you're adopted." I would ask my parents if it was true. Being too busy to take the question seriously, they would roll their eyes and say "Honey, what do you think?" The older I got, the more I saw how ridiculous my family was and the more I started to fantasize about being adopted. When, not if, one of my siblings did something incredibly stupid, I would just quietly say to myself, "Well, I don't have those genes running through me so I am in no way related to that stupidity." I stopped asking my parents for fear they would tell me the truth. Proof! My fantasy would disappear in the snap of a finger.

For those of you who have an "oops baby" or are one, I will say Brenda turned out to be a godsend. She single-handedly kept my parents young. My sister was a great athlete growing up, so my parents went to all her basketball games in high school and attended all her college track meets.

Now, my parents have lived through a lot, seen a lot and experienced a lot, but if you ask them to describe their favorite day, they will tell the story of Brenda's track team coming to Iowa to run at a local college. After the meet, the bus full of athletes pulled up in front of their home. The bus happened to be the exact length of their house. My parents had everything set up in the garage: tables, chairs, drinks, food, plates and napkins. If you aren't from the Midwest, you may think this odd. But in Iowa, you tend to have significant gatherings in your garage: high school and college graduations, wedding receptions and anniversary parties. No one really knows why. Even families with big houses have parties in their garage. With this bus load of kids there was no way Mom could have sat everyone inside the house. Fifty kids, four coaches and one bus driver piled out of the bus and formed a food line. The line stretched outside the garage and down the driveway. The chatter and laughter was deafening. Just the way my parents like it. Brenda's teammates were very appreciative and my parents were thrilled to have so much excitement and laughter at the house again. All this thanks to a cold February night in 1972.

Then Brenda started getting hard to live with and taking it over the top. Senior year, she was voted homecoming queen at Loras College. My parents were over the moon. Every time I called to check in with the folks the conversation started, "You won't believe what Brenda did…"

All of my siblings love Brenda for different reasons but I love her because she says sweet things to me like, "Don't lose hope that you really might be adopted. You are nothing like the rest of us. You're patient and a good listener. You're super smart. You're quiet and calm. Yet, oddly, the funniest sibling. You don't need constant attention. You don't have ADHD like the rest of us. It's really weird. What if your real birth parents *are* Goldie Hawn and Kurt Russell?"

Here I am, sitting on "Mom's" lap wondering when Goldie and Kurt are coming back to get me from this "fake family" photo shoot.

Okay. To be honest, I have completely embraced the fact that this is my family. Obviously, from the looks of the photo, I have yet to embrace the "Don't take life too seriously as tomorrow isn't promised" mantra. Going around the horn: Theresa, Dad, Mom, Rick, Marty, Me, David and Sherri Ann. "Mom" is all happy thinking she's done having kids. Little does she know five years and a really cold February night will change all that.

Little did I know that my parents were living their mantra. I mean *really* living it. They would live it intensely every day for five years and every day after that. Do you see my dad holding Sherri Ann's hand? Mom and Dad's favorite child? Sherri Ann.

Ok. Enough already. I think I have made it clear Brenda was sweet. However, while I have this opportunity, I do want to point out Brenda wasn't always this sweet.

I think I can say with 100% certainty that most babies of a family have one thing in common.

They need attention. Lots of it.

They love it.

Thrive on it.

Must have it.

One time I was supposed to be babysitting her (aka completely absorbed in her, playing endless games with her, entertaining her, listening to her play the trombone and telling her it was good) but instead I was in the basement engrossed in my homework and completely ignoring her.

Suddenly I hear her yelling from the top of the basement stairs. I put my book down and walk over to the stairs and look up. There she is, standing at the top of the stairs, waving a long, sharp knife around like she is conducting an orchestra. She has my full attention.

Brenda: "Play with me! You are supposed to *PAAAHHHLLLLAAAAYYYYY* with me!"

Me: "Hey crazy. Put the knife down and we will play some cards." In my head I add, "Right after you are released from the psych ward, and that episode just confirmed I am definitely adopted."

Brenda: "Ha! I knew the knife trick would work!"

Okay, maybe not all babies of families go to those extremes to get attention. And, to her credit, Brenda did keep begging me not to tell Mom and Dad on her.

Again, the baby gets what she wants. I never did tell on her. Until just now.

Here she is begging me to swim with her while I was trying to blow my candles out on my birthday cake.

Her present to mc on my 40th? Death by squeezing.

UNconventional Tip #3

Crying Wolf Could Kill You

My parents grew up during the Depression. Divorce was not an option, with them being Catholic and raising so many kids that we took up one entire pew in church. My dad worked three jobs; my mom stayed home with us and later was a lunchroom lady at our grade school just to "get out of the house." My parents were very frugal. They would never, ever spend money on frivolous things like new clothes (that's what garage sales are for), hotels (that's what camping is for), or calling an ambulance. Fast-forward through fifty-six years of marriage.

Dad was having some health issues one year. He kept feeling like he was having a heart attack. We spent many nights in the emergency room trying to figure out what was wrong. Unfortunately for my dad, the doctors couldn't quite put their fingers on the problem so Mom thought Dad was crying wolf.

Phone rings.

Dad: "Carol, I'm having a heart attack. Can you come take me to the hospital?"

Me: "Dad, hang up and call 9-1-1. I'll meet you down there."

Dad: "No, they'll charge me like it's a limo ride. I'd rather be robbed by a blind man. Can you come?"

Me: "Dad, have Mom take you. That would be a lot faster."

Dad: "Your mom just poured herself a Pepsi and lit a cigarette and she wants to finish it first."

Ten minutes later I arrive at my parents' house. Mom, sipping an ice-cold Pepsi and puffing on a cig, stationed at her designated spot at one end of the table with her feet propped up on a stool, greets me as if this is a social call.

Mom: "Hi honey! It's good to see you! Come sit down."

Me: "Dad, you look awful."

Pale Dad, sweating like Richard Simmons to the Oldies and breathing heavy, was posted at his reserved place at the other end of the table. He pants to me, "I feel awful. Thank God you're here. Your mother is refusing to take me to the hospital."

Me: "Mom, this looks serious this time. Why didn't you drive Dad?"

Mom: "Jerry, Jerry, Jerry. It's always about Jerry. The man can't go five minutes without attention. He's like a child, Carol. Really! We take him to the hospital, doctors don't know shit. They stand around and scratch their asses and then we come home. Just thought I might sit it out this time."

Me: "Um…Mom, Dad looks bad."

Mom: "Well, if he'd lose 80 pounds he wouldn't be out of breath coming up the stairs. He just walked up the stairs, honey. That's what this is all about. But your dad doesn't like to talk about losing weight. Do you, Jerry?" She emphasizes her point by looking at my dad with disgust. "Honey, come sit down. Tell me something funny my grandkids did."

Dad: "The only reason I walked upstairs is because I didn't want to die down there. I knew it would be years before you came looking for me."

Me: "Dad, get into my car. We are going to the emergency room."

Mom: "Hold your horses. Let me put out my cig and grab my coat. My Pepsi is gonna be watered down by the time I get back. Honey, can you grab it and put it in a paper cup for me? I'd hate to waste it. It's like throwing money down the damn drain."

Turned out my dad wasn't crying wolf. He was having irregular heartbeats that were causing heart attack-like symptoms (faintness, shortness of breath and sweating). So they had to perform a catheter ablation to stop the irregular heartbeats.

Unfortunately for Dad, they had to go into his groin area. Ouch.

UNconventional Tip #4

Be Farm Tough

Okay, so my mother, Colleen Virginia Reilly, is not the most empathetic person but she is the toughest woman I know. Farm tough. She's not scared of anything because she has pretty much lived through everything. Her mom was a Reilly and her father a Kelly. She is 100% Irish and proud of it. Growing up, St. Patrick's Day in our home was a sacred holiday. Mom would start early and play her Irish records from sunrise until late into the evening. She was coated in green from head to toe. The night before, my parents used to park a car along the parade route so they would have a perfect spot to watch the floats go by. I never saw Mom happier than on St. Patrick's Day. It was her day where she didn't have to buy or wrap gifts or make food for tons of people. It truly was her one day off a year. Here they are on a float in the St. Patrick's Day parade. Mom made Dad, who only had a drop of Irish in him, an honorary Leprechaun every year.

Mom grew up on a farm in Van Horne, Iowa, with eight siblings in a house with no heat. I repeat – IOWA. You know, where it snows six months of the year and where it's snowing right now as I write this.

(Not to get it confused with Idaho or Ohio like every moron I run into does. A day in an airport making small talk with people from around the world and you want to stick yourself in the eye with a pen. It should be mandatory that every adult take a mini geography quiz before they get on a plane, as they may be diverted to Iowa, Idaho, and Ohio and for the hell of it, let's throw in Illinois. Sorry, big pet peeve.)

Anyway, Mom would put a glass of water on her nightstand before bed, a bed she shared with two of her sisters, and the water would be frozen by morning.

Here's a math equation for those of you who don't have any idea what it is like to grow up on a farm in Iowa during the 1930s, 1940s and 1950s.

Farm work + no electricity + no running water = 1 tough Irish broad.

Take a moment to think of the most exhausting day you have ever experienced in your life. Now, multiply it by 10 billion and that was a typical day on the farm for my mom. Oh, and when you are done with your most exhausting day ever (joke), walk through the snow in the dead of night to the outhouse to do your business, wiping away your business with old newspapers.

ONE of Mom's mealtime jobs was to chop the heads off the chickens with a cleaver. Enough said.

If we ever made the mistake of complaining to Mom about all the chores we had to do, she would just get out the old cleaver and hold it up. There was nothing we were doing that she didn't do as a kid, and then some. We could never top Mom.

I think that by the time Mom graduated high school and left the farm she had done more work than I could ever do in a lifetime. You know what Mom called raising seven children in a home that had electricity and running water? A vacation. She had a team of children who would work for free to do her bidding.

Not only was Mom tough as nails, she was brilliant. Mom could trick us into parenting ourselves, thus avoiding the hassle of parenting whenever possible. But she also knew how to make each one of us feel special without it causing her more work.

Take birthdays for example. Nine. Every year. Ten if you count Jesus. January (Mom), February (Sherri), March (Marty), May (David), June (me), August (Theresa), October (Dad, Rick), November (Brenda) and December (Jesus). Imagine. Someone would always be celebrating a birthday. We never had the kind of outlandish birthday parties that kids have nowadays. No, Mom was too smart for that. There were no pony rides or bouncy blow-up castles that take six grown men to put together in your yard. That was for weak-minded parents who couldn't outsmart their kids. Mom, in all her glory and genius, decided that when it was your birthday, as your gift, there were two things you didn't have to do: make your bed, and clean up the kitchen after dinner.

I cannot tell you what a BIG deal this was growing up (no sarcasm intended). I felt like a queen on my birthday. It was so fun to sit in the living room on the couch, with my brilliant mom, and watch all my siblings clean up the kitchen after a big birthday dinner.

On Mother's Day my older siblings always took the lead and decided what we were doing for Mom. The longer we kept her in bed, the fewer chores we had to do that day.

One Mother's Day, Theresa and Rick, the oldest and most fearless, decided we would spoil Mom with breakfast in bed.

We had a gas stove growing up. My brother Rick was unsuccessfully trying to light the gas oven. He thought he got it, but Theresa, being older and supposedly wiser, stuck her head in it to diagnose the problem. As she was smugly telling Rick what a moron he was because he couldn't do a basic job of lighting a gas stove, Rick, who did an amazing job of tuning her out whenever she opened her mouth, decided at that moment to have another try at lighting it. This time successfully. "WWWOOOSSHH!" Theresa pulled her head out of the oven. Minus her bangs.

And eyebrows.

On that day Mom made another genius decision that would keep our family off the six o'clock news.

She emptied our house of matches and took them over to our next-door neighbor's.

UNconventional Tip #5

Size Does Matter

(According to Ole' Jer)

Two things you need to know about my dad:

1) He's an incredible salesman.
2) He's ridiculous.

Dad, when not saying outrageous and inappropriate things, is a man who can tell you the most amazing stories. At family reunions, he's the uncle all the cousins talk to because they knew they would hear a fascinating (usually true) story or a well-told joke.

Dad was a paratrooper and cook in the Army. He tells us crazy stories of jumps he made in Alaska and other locations. When skydiving became all the rage, he'd say, "Why would anyone in their right mind willingly jump out of a perfectly good airplane for fun?"

He's been a sewing machine salesman, a vacuum cleaner salesman and has run a milk truck route. Dad, many times, worked three jobs at once to support his family.

In 1972, he bought his own business called Odorite. He became known as Ole' Jer the Odorite Man. He sold deodorizers to any business that had a bathroom. These machines were put up high on a wall and had a little fan on them that pushed the fresh smells around a restroom. Each machine had his name and our address and phone number on it. He also gave away pads of paper with his slogan on it long before it was trendy. Here's a picture of one of his original pads of paper and Odorite machine.

Jerry Steepleton

OL' JER THE ODORITE MAN

My friends kidded me that my phone number
was on every bathroom wall in Iowa. His mascot

was a skunk and his slogans were "Works Well. Smells Swell." "Business Stinks But That's Good For Us!"

He would sing, "Ole' Jer the Odorite Man he cleans and sweeps the city cans!" Dad was all about the small Iowa business man. He made hundreds of friends during his thirty-odd years as the Odorite Man.

Dad taught all of us the basic techniques on how to sell well. If I wanted to go to the movies but didn't have any cash, he wouldn't just give me the money. Instead, he would make me sell home toilet deodorizers around the neighborhood. This was incredibly painful for me (for obvious reasons); however, when I came home with a few dollars for the movies, he would pick me up, spin me around and tell me how proud he was of me. At that very moment, the anxiety and sweaty armpits were well worth it.

Here I am with my Carol Brady haircut, all dolled up for the movies. But first I had to make my rounds through the neighborhood being an Odorite selling machine.

Now, the bad thing about Dad is, we will never know when he's becoming senile because he says the most inappropriate, ridiculous things and has for years. Just a sampling…

"I have gas. Pull my finger." This comment any time and any place, but especially after eating tacos.

"Some people wouldn't pay a nickel to see the Resurrection." Out loud if people are leaving mass early.

"I don't have any meat on my feet." If you are trying to decide whether you should drop Dad off at the front door of the grocery store or if you can park and both walk in together.

"I want a whoopee cushion on the kneeler in front of my casket." When my sister, Theresa, was trying to help him pick out readings and music for his funeral.

"May God strike me dead!" Whenever he tells a story to emphasize the truth of it.

"Tide detergent works great to get the grease out of hair. Why do you need shampoo?" Whenever I needed shampoo.

But this one's the kicker.

At our son, Nick's, one-year check-up, our doctor felt that it was a good idea to mention to Paul (yes, I married the man that my parents didn't think was funny) that Nick was extremely well endowed. Paul, thinking he would get some accolades for being Nick's dad and all, made the mistake of telling my dad what the doctor told him.

Dad: "Well that's no surprise. It was widely known that Colleen's brothers had the longest schlongs in Benton County. Nick's got the Reilly schlong."

Paul: "Stop saying schlong, Jerry. Am I not going to get *any* credit for this? I'm Nick's Dad."

Dad: "No, no, no. Paul, ask anyone on Colleen's side of the family, they'll tell you. Those Reilly boys were known for many things, long schlongs being one."

Paul: "Stop saying… (sigh)… I think that is THE most inappropriate and outrageous thing you have ever said."

Dad: "It's the honest-to-God truth. May God strike me dead!"

Paul: "Well, Jerry, if I was you, I'd head inside real quick. Looks like rain."

UNconventional Tip #6

Play Games With Your Parents

Speaking of God striking my dad dead, the day came when he needed to have a pacemaker put in. I picked up Mom and Dad on the morning of Dad's surgery. He was unusually quiet, which meant he was a little nervous. Mom was being extremely loving, caring and thoughtful towards Dad - another red flag. She was making sure he had packed his toothbrush, and other incidentals like grabbing the paper in case he wanted to read it later. Wow! Mom had her game face on. Now I was nervous.

I desperately wanted to make Dad laugh to lighten the mood. We have a game we play, but it didn't seem like the right time. It's called Good News/Bad News.

It goes like this:

Me: "Dad, Good News/Bad News?"

Dad: "Good News."

Me: "There will be a person from Southwest Airlines waiting for you and Mom with wheelchairs to take you to your gate so you can make your connecting flight on time."

Dad: "Yippee! Carol, thanks for taking care of that. You know we can't walk very far. I don't have any meat on my feet (again with the meat on the feet comment). Bad News?"

Me: "You have to tip them."

But I followed Mom's cue and played it straight. No cracking jokes or making silly comments or playing Good News/Bad News. Dad is over six feet tall, but a good 80 pounds overweight. Definitely not the most fit individual going in for a procedure. You could cut the tension in the air with a knife. The drive to the hospital was quiet. Normally I would have loved that, but not today.

During some of the nurse prep work, Dad started to relax a little. This was a good sign. The time was right for some Good News/Bad News.

Dad: "Carol, remember, if anything should happen, I don't want to go to a nursing home."

This was Dad *discreetly* letting me know that he and Mom want to live with me and never go into a nursing home.

Me: "Good News/Bad News."

Dad: "Good."

Me: "Dad, I promise that when the time comes, I would never put you in a nursing home."

Dad: "Okay. Good girl. You're my favorite daughter (a bold-faced lie, as we all know Sherri Ann's his favorite). I don't tell you that enough. Bad?"

Me: "Mom and I have talked it over and when that time comes, I'm going to smother you with a pillow instead. She doesn't think she'd be strong enough to hold you down. No, no. You don't have to thank me. I'm happy to help."

After the surgery, which went like clockwork, Mom was back to herself.

Mom: "Honey, I'm heading to the cafeteria for a Pepsi. I can't take another minute in this room. It's too stuffy. God only knows when your father is going to wake up. It probably took an oil tanker of anesthesia to put him out."

Me: "I'll stay. You take a break."

It wasn't much later and Dad was slowly coming around. I have never been with anyone coming out of anesthesia. Dad would open his eyes and look around then fall back to sleep for a few minutes. Then wake up again. He would mumble something then sleep again for a bit. I got up out of my chair and stood next to the bed. I was holding his hand. He opened his eyes and was wetting his lips like he was going to talk some more so I bent my head down close to his face.

Dad: "Carol, where am I?"

Me: "Good News/Bad News."

Dad: "Bad."

Me: "We're in hell."

Dad: "Good?"

Me: "I'm just visiting."

I can still hear his laugher. It was a beautiful sound.

UNconventional Tip #7

Marry A Man In A Speedo

You know what else is a beautiful sound? The garage door opening when my husband gets home from a business trip. He has traveled for all but three of our married years. I followed my parents' advice and married someone who made me laugh.

Remember that guy from chapter one who had given me a promise ring with a diamond the size of a grain of sand and who had to listen to my dad lecture him about blue balls? That's Paul. We like to call him Mr. Safety. Paul makes a complete stop at every stop sign, always uses his blinker, never cuts his toe nails too short, is constantly blowing out my candles and is not a fan of pumpkin carving or anything to do with knives. Bungee jumping, skydiving or rock climbing will never make his bucket list. However, I have to give Mr. Safety credit. He still encourages our kids to follow their dreams, even if those dreams are things he would never do. When our son started flying planes he would call home with stories like, "My instructor killed my engine today and I had to land without one. I did it, but slid sideways down the runway." Paul would listen and say all the right things, then hang up and put his hands on his head and silently shake his head in disbelief. Sometimes for hours.

Here's a picture of Paul when our daughter told us she was going to India with other medical students to observe surgeries and learn dental procedures.

Poor Paul couldn't stop saying, "India? Why India? Could someone please explain to me why India? We have people in America with bad teeth!"

Paul and I tend to balance each other out when it comes to taking things too seriously. In our early twenties, a conversation while riding bikes would go like this...

Paul: "We need to plan for our retirement and treat it like a bill coming in the mail every month. We will take $100 right off the top of what we make and put it into an aggressive long-term investment. We'll do the same for our kids' college tuition the minute they are born."

Carol: "I like riding my ten speed no-handed."

I periodically have grandiose ideas. Paul knows how to rein me in, keeping me grounded, but still be encouraging. After watching an IMAX film about Mt. Everest, we are walking to our car and I announce, with complete conviction, that I will be climbing Mount Everest within the year. Paul looks at me, smiles, reaches for my hand, holds it tight and says, "I know that if you put your mind to it, you could climb Mt. Everest. But, you do realize there are no chips, salsa and margaritas waiting for you at the top of Mount Everest, right? Why don't we join a health club and work out together instead?"

We've been married 27 years and yes, he's since upgraded my promise ring. He is a very sincere and practical man and a great father, and is actually very funny (forget what my parents say), although many times unknowingly.

The part of Paul's brain that makes sound financial decisions, great parenting choices, and can find the parking space farthest away from the door we need to go into works brilliantly, but the part of his brain that makes proper clothing choices is lagging about 15 years behind. I am going to make this clear: I did not marry a fashionista.

Here's Paul with his sharp-looking dad, Don, who knew to insert some solid-color clothing choices into his wardrobe. I would have been on high alert had this picture surfaced during our courtship. Obviously, Paul's mom had it on lockdown mode.

Paul and I met at Loras College in Dubuque, Iowa. He was a sophomore and I was a freshman.

He was on the golf team and liked to run. I didn't know what golf was and I avoided running anywhere. But somehow we hit it off and started dating.

On a Saturday during the first summer of our courtship, Paul and I decided to meet at Palo Beach. Up to this point, all clothing had remained on during our dates so my view of his body had been limited. Obviously, I was somewhat aware he was fit and had an ass that could be used as a butt double in a movie. But I had yet to see the entire picture. I knew it was time for the "beach date", which would allow me to cut my losses and check out before I was too invested in this guy.

It was a sunny, perfect day. I was excited to see what he would look like in his swimsuit. We kissed hello and removed our shorts and tank tops and settled in for a day of making out in the water. I turned away from Paul to lay my towel on my beach chair, and when I turned back I couldn't believe my eyes.

Me: "What are you wearing?"

Paul: "What?"

Me: "Is that the only swimsuit you brought?"

Paul: "It's the only swimsuit I own."

I was at a pivotal moment in my life. My brain was saying, "Pack up and leave. Don't look back. You are dating a man COMPLETELY out of touch with reality and fashion and if you make a life together your future is going to be full of frustration, embarrassment…and lots of laughter." I stayed put. I love to laugh.

Me: "You realize that most men in the free world are wearing board shorts for a swimsuit."

Paul: "Those are outrageous." (Paul has yet to learn the proper use of the word outrageous.) "They only come in loud colors and they're so long they go past my knees. You can't even swim in them, and if you try they cling to your legs and drip for hours."

Me: "Oh – THOSE swimsuits are outrageous? THOSE swimsuits? Paul! You are wearing a BABY BLUE SPEEDO!"

Paul: "Isn't it great? I can actually swim in this. Did you know I was on the swim team?"

Me: "YES! When you were twelve! That thing barely contains your package! It's straining against the little material that's holding it in, begging to breathe and break free. For God's sakes wrap a towel around yourself!"

Paul: "Oh, that's your fault. It wasn't doing that when I put it on this morning."

Hmmm….it was good to know all systems were go. The one beautiful thing about Paul wearing the speedo? He wasn't wearing it to be risqué. He was wearing it because he's practical and wanted to swim. That's what makes Paul, Paul. And makes the rest of us laugh.

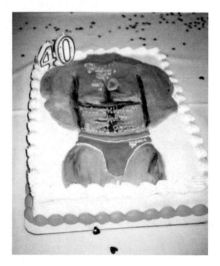

Here's the cake I designed to celebrate Paul's 40th birthday.

A prequel to "Baby Blue".

The speedo was just the beginning. Paul has a habit of pulling his pants up way too high. In spite of the countless times I'd adjust Paul's pants to have them stay on his waist, they always seemed to be kissing his armpits. Have you ever seen the Shoebox Hallmark card that has a picture of a man with his pants pulled up to his neck? The punchline goes something like, "At least you save money on shirts this way." Over the years, Paul has received that birthday card no less than twenty times from his friends and family.

Me: "Paul, your pants aren't touching your shoes."

Paul: "Oh, you're right."

He adjusts his pants downward. He makes one move, say to put a plate in the dishwasher, and the pants go right back up to his armpits. Like a baby to the breast every time. So I have come to understand that Paul's armpits are just a natural resting place for the tops of his pants.

I know it sounds like I am exaggerating but I'm not. Not even close.

My friend, Liz, met Paul for the very first time one evening when a group of couples were gathering at a restaurant. Pleasantries and handshakes all around and great dinnertime conversation was had by all. Afterward, she says to me, "Great to meet Johnny High Pockets. Loved looking at his package all tight up against his jeans. There is no way he's stuffing his pants with socks,

right? Is all that for real? Sista you got it going ON!
Congrats!"

UNconventional Tip #8

Visit Possible Future In-Laws

Paul and I were raised completely differently by our respective parents. I had a million chores to do each day before I could play outside. I always wanted to play outside due to the limited size of the house and the unlimited amount of noise. Dusting, vacuuming, cleaning bathrooms, washing dishes (until the big day we got a dishwasher that was portable and hooked up to the kitchen sink), laundry and dessert-making were just a few of my chores. I also made my parents' bed every morning.

Paul's chores growing up were limited. He had never used a washer or dryer, dishwasher, cleaned a toilet or cooked on a stove. When I met Paul he had purple khakis. I didn't know they made purple khakis. I asked where he got them and he said they used to be tan, but he washed them with his navy blue khakis and now they were purple. His lack of experience with laundry was an issue. He blew it one night back in his dorm room. I stopped by to say hi, and he invited me to have a seat on his bunk but I noticed the sheets looked a weird color of gray. I asked when was the last time he washed his sheets, and he said he hadn't yet. It was March. School had been in session for seven months. I started backing out of the room saying, "Hey, I have an exam I just remembered I have to study for. See ya later."

Not only were we raised differently, our environments growing up were extreme opposites. My house was like a football stadium with the constant hum of noise accompanied by giant roars. You never got to finish a sentence, people were always talking over the top of each other and constantly interrupting each other, food disappeared the minute it was placed on the table, and of course there was a lot of cussing, usually by my parents.

What I remember most about the first time I walked into Paul's home was the quiet. I should have anticipated it. He never mentioned the level of noise in his house growing up but there were subtle signs. I wouldn't call Paul a soft talker but he was close. If I interrupted him while talking he looked at me all confused, like I had grown three heads. He would stand there, dazed, let me finish interrupting him and then announce, "As I was saying..." During the evening of our very first date, Paul kept saying to me, "Do you realize you're talking really loud?"

He would continue to say it in different ways throughout the night so as not to make me feel bad. "It's not very loud in the restaurant, you don't have to use your outdoor voice...you do realize you were not whispering during the movie, right?... perhaps you've been swimming and your ears are plugged...I'm right here" and so on. Even though it didn't seem like I was speaking loudly, it all made sense after stepping into his childhood home.

It was amazing. Quiet. Peaceful. Like a sanctuary. I could hear some soft piano music playing in the background. I kept waiting for a woman to come take me through to the back for the first of my many spa treatments.

Dinner time with Paul's parents and family was like sitting down with the Waltons, but with only three kids. People passed food counter-clockwise, said please and thank you and actually listened to each other. No one interrupted while someone else was talking. It was surreal.

After dinner, we moved into the living room and continued visiting in normal indoor voices. The sound was soothing. Paul interrupted my trance-like state by telling his parents goodbye. I didn't want to ever leave.

The conversation in the car back to college went like this:

Me: "Your mom and dad didn't swear the entire day."

Paul: "No."

Me: "Your parents are quiet and respectful to each other."

Paul: "Yes."

Me: "Why are you dating me?"

Paul: "Because you're nothing like your family."

Me: "Why else?"

Paul: "Because I think you might actually be adopted which would make it biologically impossible to be anything like your family."

Me: "Any other reason?"

Paul: "You're unconventional and you make me laugh."

Bam! There it was! Thanks Mom and Dad.

UNconventional Tip #9

Timing Is Everything

Speaking of thanking my parents, doctors had found polyps in my dad's colon and because of that, my doctor asked me to have a colonoscopy at age 45 instead of 50. No big deal. I'm a very optimistic person by nature. I had heard this procedure was a breeze. I was not worried...until Paul told me some news.

I was prepping the night before when Paul announced he had to leave the hospital during my test to meet with a client, but it would only take about thirty minutes.

Me: "The hospital insists that someone I know is in the hospital at all times during my procedure in case anything goes wonky."

Paul: "I'll be able to take you and be with you during prep, but I will have to leave. I'll be back to pick you up long before you are done. I'll have your parents come sit at the hospital while I'm gone."

I start shaking my head no, my mouth gapes open and I am in complete shock! Paul must have missed the line in our marriage contract that reads: *I hereby declare said husband is not allowed to let said wife's parents attend any procedure that takes place at a hospital.*

Unless your procedure is life or death, my parents tend to be a little nuts when they are in a hospital. Nothing is off-limits. They are taunters. You are wasting their time if you are at the hospital and not dying.

Me: "Oh my God, if you had given me some notice I would have used a lifeline and phoned a friend. You need to make this right. Do you hear me? Timing is everything here. I would really rather not see my parents before the procedure! I am using my loud voice, Paul, so please note that I mean business!"

Paul: "Loud and clear, Captain. I will call your parents and handle this. I will let them know the *exact* time to be there, down to the minute. You just relax and go drink your orange liquid that makes it impossible for me to come within fifty feet of our bathroom."

The next day Paul and I are walking into the hospital and my parents are already there, drinking coffee and talking to complete strangers about their personal health issues. This exact scenario would also be duplicated in the checkout line at any grocery store, in an elevator or anywhere else you may be stuck with my parents for a few minutes and can't walk away.

Me: Fake smile as I greet my parents.

Mom: "What the hell are you doing with that smile on your face? Don't you have any idea what they are going to do to you today?" She laughs hard.

Really hard. She grabs her cane and sits back down. She's off-balance from all of her belly laughing.

Me: "My friend, Gwen, is an endoscopy (butt and gut) nurse and she said this is no big deal. Really, it's just another opportunity to take my pants off."

Mom: "Okay, honey. Believe what you want." Giggles.

Me (through clenched teeth): "What are you both doing down here so early? You don't have to be here for another hour and a half."

Dad: "What else do we have to do? It's nice knowing we're here just in case one of us starts to have a heart attack."

Mom: "Did you drink all that orange shit from the gallon jug last night? Awful, awful stuff."

Me: "Yes, I managed it just fine." I didn't want to tell her I threw up about halfway through the gallon.

Dad: "Carol and Paul, come meet (fill in stranger's name here). He's waiting for (fill in family member's name here) to get out of (fill in random procedure here)."

Me: "Dad, I need to find the admitting nurse. I don't have time to meet your random new hospital friends right now."

I meet with the nurse and sign the papers. She opens the big double doors to let Paul and me through to the prep rooms.

Dad, yelling now because we are headed down the hallway and doors are starting to close, "You're going to be farting like a dog when you're done in there!"

Mom, chiming in and of course yelling, "Those doctors are going to wipe that smile right off your face in a hurry! You won't be smiling for long! Have fun!"

I glance at the nurse. She's cringing.

I look back. Both of my parents are laughing and waving at me as the remote control double doors close in their faces. I turned to Paul. "Well, that went well."

Paul: "Yeah. Your mom should be a motivational speaker."

UNconventional Tip #10

Lie To Your Parents

My family and friends will tell you I am the most honest person they know. But there does come a time in your life where lying is mandatory.

I don't know about you, but I am not perfect. I am not super mom or super wife or super anything. Granted, there are lots of things I have tried to be super at and failed. Clipping coupons is one of them. But I am super great about *lying* to my dad about clipping coupons.

Obviously, feeding a ridiculously large family is fairly expensive. Dad and Mom knew how to make a dollar stretch like a new egg of Silly Putty. If I had a nickel for every time my parents told me to go pick some dollars off the money tree in the backyard I would be rich. Dad was always saying, "I wish I was as rich as my kids." When I was growing up, my parents would hand me the newspaper and tell me to clip out any coupon for a product that we use. I would tag along with Dad as we went from store to store saving money. I was also the sole stamp-licker for the S & H green stamps book. This was a program where you earn stamps from supermarkets, department stores, gas stations and other retailers. You lick the stamps and put them in books and then you redeem the books for products out of a catalog. I would always assume that once the books were full I would get to pick the prize (since I did all the work), so I had my eye on some cool roller skates and a pogo stick. Mom would remind me it was Dad's money that bought the product that got the stamps that I licked. So a blender or a mixer or some other helpful kitchen product would arrive, compliments of my stamp-licking.

Fast-forward twenty-five years.

Not a day goes by where Dad does not call me and tell me where all the good bargains are around town. "Aldi's has hamburger for twenty-five cents a pound. Unbelievable! Don't buy hamburger anywhere else today. It would be a damn sin. Gas is two dollars and sixteen cents at Sinclair. Stop what you are doing and go gas up. You never know when those bastards are going to change the prices. K-mart has toilet paper on sale. Coupon's on the sixth page of section C in the paper. It's like they're giving it away today. It's going fast. Everyone uses TP. Even John Wayne uses TP. You can always use extra TP." Dad would call multiple times a day about coupons, bargains and someone that he knew who showed up on the obituary page that day. But here's the kicker. My parents would *not* call me about mouth-dropping events. One Saturday I had fielded about three calls from Dad regarding meat on sale. That night Paul and I are driving over to their house. We are one block away when we see a house smoldering from a fire that evidently just got put out a few hours before. A *FIRE*! A house was on fire *four* houses from my parents' house and guess what? *NO PHONE CALL*! We pull into the driveway and my parents are sitting out on their patio. You can still smell the smoke in the air.

Me: "Hey, Mom and Dad, anything new in the neighborhood?"

Dad: "Well, our neighbors can't keep their damn dog in their yard. If I have to pick up poop one more time I'm calling the damn cops."

Me: "Dad, please don't call the cops about poop. Anything else happening that we should know about?"

Mom: "The little gal across the street and her husband are going to have a baby."

Me (exasperated at this point): "What about the house that burned down four houses from you?"

Mom: "Oh, that. They think it was a meth lab."

Anyway, what my dad didn't know was that my coupon-clipping days were over. I tried. I really did. I would clip and then couldn't remember where I put them. Once, I actually clipped the coupons and put them in my purse and then forgot to use them at the checkout line. I was waiting in line saying this mantra over and over in my head: "Don't forget the coupons. Don't forget the coupons. Don't forget the coupons." But as soon as I started removing food from the shopping cart, that was my kids' cue to remove all the candy off of those convenient little shelves and put it on the conveyer belt while I was reaching underneath for all the heavy stuff I had jammed under the cart. So then I would be telling the checkout person that I didn't want that pound of Laffy Taffy or fifteen packs of Bubblicious Bubble Gum. By the time it was all said and done, I would be exhausted and pushing my extremely heavy cart, holding my kids' hands and trying to reach into my purse for my keys...and then I'd see my coupons all paper-clipped together, staring back at me and screaming, "Why do you even try?"

So I don't any more. I just own it. "Hi. My name's Carol. I'm not a coupon-clipper." I have completely removed that from my list of things to be good at.

But, here's another kicker. I never told Dad. I would just play along and be like, "Hellz yeah, I'm heading to Aldi's as we speak! There better damn well be some hamburger left over by the time I get there!" I lied for years about clipping coupons and obediently store-hopping for meat, canned goods and bathroom products that were on sale. I was even buying all my bathroom products at the (gulp!) grocery store. But what I lost in money I saved in time. Dragging kids around from store to store lost its appeal quickly.

My coupon non-compliance plan worked great until the day I got busted.

Coupon-Gate (as Paul likes to refer to it) happened as I was pulling into my driveway after a grocery store run. Dad was waiting in his car. He had called earlier in the day and said he was going to stop over with extra Pillsbury crescent roll coupons. He offered to help me carry my stuff in. I tried to tell him no and asked him to just go inside and pour us each a glass of wine. He wouldn't hear of it. So I opened the back door of my truck and there were all my grocery bags.

Dad: "Well, lookie here. You went to Hy-Vee. I wish I was as rich as my kids."

We get the bags inside and Kate and Nick start going through sacks to find their Tic Tacs (I can't say no to mints). Dad is standing at the kitchen island where food and products are now thrown asunder. Dad picks up a box of 200-count tissue.

Dad: "What the hell is this? Did you buy Kleenex at *Hy-Vee*?" He is using the same voice he would use if he was saying, "You posed naked for *WHAT* magazine?"

I hang my head in shame.

Dad: "You didn't even have a coupon, did you? I taught you better than this, Carol. What the hell's the matter with you? Have some pride, girl! You know better than to buy Kleenex at a grocery store! You just flushed $1.50 down the toilet. That is what you did. You flushed Paul's hard-earned $1.50 down the toilet. That's a damn shame. A damn shame I tell you."

Me (composing myself before I lay a big one on Dad): "Just a moment of weakness, Dad. The kids and I have been sick and I haven't been able to get out with them. I was tired of blowing my nose with toilet paper and the Kleenex was right there so I grabbed a box. Sorry I let you down."

Dad, still holding the Kleenex box at arm's length like it is a dirty diaper: "Okay…well…we all have our moments. Let's not tell Paul about this. The man works too damn hard."

UNconventional Tip #11

Marriage Is Not For Wimps

I love Paul dearly but there were times in our marriage (like all marriages) where frustration would set in. One such time was about six years into our marriage; "the honeymoon was over", we had yet to have children and we were both very independent and busy with our jobs. Every now and again I would call Mom to complain about Paul. Correction. This only happened once. I quickly learned that the division of household duties and standards for today's husbands versus a husband back in the 40's and 50's were a little different.

I dialed Mom.

Mom: "Hi Honey!"

Me: "Hi Mom."

Mom: "What's the matter, Honey? You sound down."

Me: "I feel taken for granted. I don't think Paul appreciates me. I work over 40 hours a week, do all the cooking and cleaning around here, grocery and Target shopping too. Paul just works and plays golf."

Mom: "Honey, I'm confused. Does Paul beat you?"

Me: "What? No, of course not. What do you mean?"

Mom: "Does he lay hands on you?"

Me: "Mom! Of course not."

Mom: "Does he drink too much or do drugs? Is he having sex with other women without trying to hide it?"

Me: "MOM! NO! That is *crazy*! Of course he isn't doing those things."

Mom: "Well, Honey. Marriage is not for wimps. We are fortunate. We have husbands that don't do those things. Plus, you have a roof over your head and clothes on your back. What more could you ask for?"

Me: "Mom, I help pay for the roof and clothes. I am asking for help with the cleaning, cooking and shopping. Thank goodness he knows how to do his own laundry."

Mom: "*WHAT?* Honey, there are machines that help you do those things now. Why is Paul doing his own laundry? The man has a job for God's sakes. Why would Paul help with *YOUR* chores? Carol, that is just laziness on your part. L – A – Z – Y." Mom would spell out the words in a singsongy voice. "Paul needs to go golfing to get rid of the stress of his job. Don't call me to complain about Paul. He sounds like a dream. Take my advice. Hang up this phone and get on your knees and thank the good Lord above that you have the husband you do."

Click.

Lesson learned. Save complaining about your husband for your girlfriends who got married in the same decade as you.

UNconventional Tip #12

Avoid FCS

When I discovered I was pregnant with Kate, naturally I was a little concerned. Questions flowed in abundance from my head. Did I have the tools I needed to be a good mom? Would I be patient and loving? Would I be smart enough to help them with physics and calculus junior year? (I actually already knew the answer to this question but I didn't want to admit it just yet.)

Something I will admit is that I had **First Child Syndrome** and I had it bad. FCS is where you think you are the only woman in the world who can raise a child properly and you have all the answers because you have seen countless other mothers doing it *all* wrong. At Walmart, at the doctor's office, at restaurants.

Take playing in the snow with your child.

Growing up with Midwest winters makes you tough. You play in the snow wearing a t-shirt, jeans and gloves (for making snowballs). I don't think my mom ever bought any of us a snowsuit. (Wait…my sister, Brenda, got a snowsuit. Makes sense.) Mom would half-heartedly ask us to wear our winter coats, knowing that in about five minutes they would be unzipped and laying in a snow pile or being used as a sled. I don't remember NOT having fun in the snow as a kid. Some of my greatest memories are of snow days: sledding, snowball fights, snowman-making contests, snow angels, building snowball forts and igloos. But, when you have a child, you forget about all the fun you had and you just want them to be safe and warm. What if an icicle falls off the roof and splits open their skull? I'm sorry I think like this but I am married to Mr. Safety, who will go through every dangerous scenario of what could have happened but didn't. He has warped my mind a little. So what do I do? I forget about my wonderful childhood playing in the snow and start saying things like, "Gosh, I could have gotten frostbite growing up. Why didn't my mom insist I wear a coat and hat?" Naturally, I would come to the conclusion that she didn't love me. FCS strikes with a vengeance and with disastrous results. I created a daughter who really didn't like to play in the snow. Why? 'Cause she couldn't move. She wasn't going to get to experience all of the fun I had growing up, because I dressed her like an oompa-loompa and all she would do is waddle around the yard, periodically fall over and be unable to get back up.

Thank goodness FCS weakens with wisdom. Eventually, thoughts like "Maybe Mom was onto something" saved me money on winter gear, and eventually Kate stopped hiding from me when it snowed.

UNconventional Tip #13

"Free" Babysitting Isn't Free

Now, I know it sounds like Paul isn't a huge fan of my family, but the truth is this: he loves my family. It was actually his idea to move and be closer to my family. We have been fortunate to live in the same town as my parents for most of our children's lives. And Paul's parents are a quick two-hour drive away in Keokuk, Iowa. My kids have benefited immensely from having their grandparents in their lives.

Our parents are typical grandparents in that they adore their grandchildren. My dad always said, "Grandkids are a gift from God for not killing your teenagers."

If I try at all to complain about my kids, Mom jumps all over it. She takes examples of rotten behavior exhibited by my brothers and sisters and uses it against me.

Me: "Nick has started biting Kate when she's not listening to him."

Mom (totally dismissing my comments with a wave of her hand): "They're angels, Carol. *ANGELS* I tell you."

Me: "Mom, biting is bad."

Mom: "No, filling a kickball with gasoline, lighting the kickball on fire, yelling '*Halley's Comet*' then kicking it at your brother's head is bad. Have five more kids and biting won't even register on your radar."

Interjecting a TBT photo here. It is actually Thursday when I am writing this so it's legit. Notice my brother, Marty, on the right side of picture, holding said kickball Mom was referring to (currently not containing gasoline).

My other brother, David, is telling me to "Keep my hands in the air and hit the deck!" As you can see, I was quick to comply. I am going to assume Mom was taking a smoke break when this picture was going down.

Now, to my brothers' credit, they could be very well behaved. They look like angels on that step. And they rarely picked their nose. Unlike me.

Anyway, I thought for sure that living in the same town as my parents would reap another key reward. Free babysitting.

Not.

My kids were about seven and five when Mom offered to come to my house to watch them while I ran some errands. If my parents offered to babysit my kids, I usually took them to my parents' house because it was just easier on Mom and Dad. This was not easier on me, however, because I had to haul all their crap over to my parents' house because there was nothing in their house for my kids to play with. I soon learned this was really stupid of me because they never played with the toys I brought over. They would play with an old refrigerator box they found in the basement, an old pogo stick that was missing a spring that Dad kept saying he would fix, or the set of stilts I wouldn't let my parents throw out in case I ever decided to join the circus. It would take me an hour to pack up their stuff, haul it over there and unload it. Only to repack it a couple of hours later and haul it back to my house to unload it. It was just less exhausting to hire a babysitter. So when Mom offered to come over to my house to watch the kids I jumped at the chance.

I have a craft closet that rivals Hobby Lobby with shelves and shelves of craft materials: paints, paper, colors, markers, popsicle sticks, glue, glitter, pipe cleaners. You name it. I had it. Every day I made sure my kids had a couple of hours of craft time. My kids totally got into it and were (bragging alert) very creative.

Me: "Mom, I saved craft time for while I am gone, so you can just sit at the table and help them create. Easy peasy. I'll be back in a couple of hours."

About two hours later I returned home to find Mom sound asleep on the living room couch, and my kids playing with hand-crafted bows and arrows made from wire hangers and sharpened pencils. They had cut slits in the erasers and slid the notched-out erasers onto the hanger with the sharpened end of the pencil being the tip of their arrow. A pillow was on a chair being used as a target. (As opposed to each other, thank you Jesus).

One decision every new parent has to make is whether to allow toy weapons in their house. I married Mr. Safety, so it was agreed our kids would not be playing with toy weapons and I knew this was not going to go over big. Little did we know just *how* creative our very creative kids were. (Jumping ahead ten years, we also didn't know we would cave, and airsoft guns and Nerf guns would be strewn all around our house.)

My kids were demonstrating their new weapons to me when Mom woke up. She sits up and wipes the drool off her face. She watches Kate shoot the pencil across the room and sees it land just short of the pillow. She looks at me a little horrified.

Nick: "Let me twhy! Let me twhy!" (Nick's speech lessons had yet to start kicking in.)

Mom: "Carol, I'm a little surprised you let your kids play with such dangerous toys. You know Paul is not going to like that one bit."

Me: "Mom, the kids made these while you were napping."

Now, Mom never, ever, *EVER* admitted that she took a nap. Let alone fell sound asleep. She would have pillow crease marks on her face that took hours to disappear, but would be adamant she was only resting her eyes. Naps were for weak people.

Mom: "Impossible. I only rested my eyes for a few minutes. They must have had those stashed somewhere, like maybe under their beds. Kids are always putting crap they don't want their parents to see under their beds. They will do it when they're teenagers, too. You need to keep a closer watch."

Me: "Kate, when did you make these?"

Kate: "While Grandma Colleen was snoring."

UNconventional Tip #14

Ignore the Crash Cart

Turns out, all that "napping" Mom was doing was a symptom of issues that were eventually going to land her in the hospital. I know I have mentioned how tough my mom is, and that is no exaggeration. Mom won't do anything she doesn't want to and has outsmarted her doctors on more than one occasion.

When Mom was hospitalized with some heart issues there was a red cart in her room. The crash cart is designed to look like a little dresser on wheels. It is a beautiful cherry red color that actually brightens up the ICU (Intensive Care Unit) room, unless you know what's inside.

Most of my siblings flew or drove in for this particular ICU stint. Granted, Mom was weak, but she was still completely aware of the situation and thoroughly enjoying holding court in her ICU room. She loved that Dad was not getting any attention. She wanted us all jammed in the room, chatting and keeping her company. She didn't say much, but followed the conversations, stories and funny jokes with nods of her head, smiles and thumbs-ups. We tried to give the ICU the respect it deserves by using quiet voices (that lasted about ten minutes) and not as many hand gestures to tell our stories. It was technically a mini family reunion. The nurse was not happy. She came in more than once and told us to quiet down. However, we all knew what Mom needed in order to heal, and we were giving it to her. At one point, one of my brothers, who can be very sensitive, started crying and Mom asked him to leave the room. She wasn't having any of it. She whispered, "No downers are allowed in my room."

About four days into her stay in the ICU, I cornered the doctor outside Mom's room.

Conversation with doctor who liked to use idioms when talking went something like this…

Me: "What's the plan? You have been talking about a pacemaker. Why aren't you making any decisions?"

Doctor: "Do you know what that red cart is?"

Me: "Crash cart."

Doctor: "You hit the nail on the head. I think you might be the only one. Everyone else in your family seems oblivious to the fact that we have the crash cart in your mom's room. Your family hasn't seen the light. They are unusually hopeful that your mom is going to rebound and actually be strong enough for surgery."

Me: "It's called faith."

Doctor: "Carol, your mom is going to play her cards and then we'll play ours. A pacemaker probably isn't going to happen. We just have to take it one day at a time."

A few days later the doctor calls my dad out into the hallway. Dad motions for me to come with.

Doctor: "Jerry, Colleen is holding her cards close to her chest. I have run out of time. These last four days she has slowly improved and is actually getting stronger. Her appetite has returned. She is forcing me to play my cards. We are going to put a pacemaker in tomorrow. She is one tough woman."

Dad and I in unison: "Tell me about it."

After the doctor has left, Dad says to me, "Funny how that doctor thinks he was in charge of this situation the whole time. You and I both know that God and Mom are always running the show, and not necessarily in that order."

UNconventional Tip #15

Play Plumber

Speaking of running the show, Paul travels each week for his work. He put his entire trust in me to raise our children so they wouldn't turn out to be hellions.

It was a tightrope. We had grown up completely differently. Paul is reserved, intelligent, soft-spoken and patient. I am...well...me (perhaps still holding out hope that my parents are Goldie and Kurt) but starting to embrace my outlandish family traits.

If I had to use one word to describe my kids it wouldn't be the usual – cute (my kids were cue balls until they were two years old) or intelligent (my kids take turns at being dumb-dumbs). The word I would use to describe my kids is observant.

Once we had a plumber to the house to fix our garbage disposal. Kate and Nick watched him. Closely. After the plumber left, Kate and Nick are coming up from the basement with balls tucked under the front of their shirts.

Me: "What's happening here?"

Kids: "We're playing plumber."

They turn and walk into the kitchen to get tools out of the tool kit I keep under the sink. When they do this I see they have their pants pulled down to show their butt cracks. I knew at that moment I was on the right path into motherhood…sort of…

The patting of myself on the back didn't last long. My son, five at the time, loved the idea that he could pull his pants down a little and not get in trouble. I had created a monster.

"Playing Plumber" eventually led to him mooning family members.

It happened quickly and caught people off-guard. He only wore sweats with elastic waistbands so it was a quick flash of blinding white and then he was gone, with belly laughter echoing off the walls as he ran down the hallway. Naturally, my parents found this hilarious and loved when they would be the recipients of a random moon.

How to solve this? What to do? Think, Carol. Think! By now my mother's wisdom had cured me of FCS, and my UTI (Unconventional Thinking Initiative) was in full force. Over the years, I discovered certain situations would arise and sometimes the only way to solve the problem was to remove my pants. This situation called for a creative pants-removal mission.

Later that same week on Friday night we had all stayed up late. Our three bedrooms are right by each other. I had tucked Kate in and was saying prayers with Nick, cuddled up in his bed with him. His baseball nightlight was plugged into the wall socket, adding just enough light to the room to make my mission possible. As I said goodnight and was walking out of the room, I mooned him. I'm not talking butt-crack moon. I'm talking full-on butt cheeks to the top of the legs moon. Then calmly walked across the hall and climbed into my bed, where Paul was already under the covers, nearly asleep.

Nick: "AUGGGHHHHH! DAD! DAD! MOM JUST MOONED ME! MOM JUST MOONED ME!"

Kate (yelling from her room): "Nick, you're a liar! Mom would never do that! You're just saying that because you moon everyone and it's gross."

Nick, out of breath from screaming so loud: "No, Kate – Dad! I am not making this up! Dad, can you hear me?"

Paul: "Nick, pipe down. Lower your voice. Your mom and I are still trying to figure out your punishment for all this mooning. Don't add lying to it."

Nick, screaming at the top of his lungs now and running out of his room: "DAD, PLEASE I'M NOT LYING. MOM. JUST. MOONED. ME! WHY IS

NO ONE BELIEVING MEEEEEEE?" I hear sniffling as Nick starts walking back to his room.

Paul: "Nick, go back to bed. It's late. You are making things worse for yourself."

Now full-on crying as he climbs back into his bed.

Paul: "Carol, you did not just moon our son, right?"

Calmly I say in the dark, "Paul, what kind of mother moons their child?"

Paul: "Sorry, I had to ask."

Attention all readers! Unconventional thinking works! Nick stopped mooning.

I, however, did not. Mooning my kids is the best unconventional parenting tip I have to share. There is nothing like the sound of a belly laugh from your child. Belly laughter is rare in their sulky teen years and almost non-existent in their early college years. I pull it out only in extreme cases when I know my child could use a good laugh.

Kate came home from college one weekend. It was the start of her second semester, and the newness of college had worn off but the dread of knowing she was going to be studying her butt off for the next three and a half years had set in. She was out of sorts and a little depressed.

I made her a yummy meal and did her laundry with her. We played some cards. She loaded the car and was saying goodbye. I walked her to her car in the driveway. It was January. The dead of winter. She gave me a big hug that lasted a lot longer than most. Now this **confirmed** she still wasn't herself because *usually* her hugging technique needs work. She is my one-armed hugger with a side lean in, but on this night she had two arms tight around me and wasn't letting go. She finally ended the embrace and got into her car. As she was backing out of the driveway she glanced back at me and I hit her with a full-on moon. She stopped the car and doubled over her steering wheel laughing. I couldn't hear her but I could see her beautiful white smile from where I stood in the garage. So worth it. Here's the text I got when she was back to her dorm: "Back at dorm. Thx 4 dinner & full moon 2nite. Ur outrageous. Love that about u."

I still keep a picture of a moon on my phone that I send to my kids when they need a good laugh and when they are taking life and themselves a little too seriously.

We all need reminding to enjoy each day we have because tomorrow isn't promised. My sister, Sherri Ann, reminds me every morning that life is fleeting and each day is a gift to enjoy.

And maybe a day to moon your kids.

UNconventional Tip #16

Work Less and Swim More

If your husband travels for a living and you stay home with the kids, you quickly realize he is white collar and you are blue collar.

You obviously handle all the children's basic needs: food, water and clothing. Plus, all the grocery shopping, Target shopping, doctor appointments, drug dealing – Nick you get the pink pill (Zithromax) and Kate you get the blue one (allergy).

I am sure you have read all the statistics on what stay-at-home moms would rake in if someone was paying them (with something other than kisses and hugs). According to a survey of more than 6,000 mothers by salary.com, the average non-working mom spends 94 hours a week juggling tasks that would earn a total salary of $113,568.

Okay – fantasy time is over. Back to reality. No salary.

How to do all this alone? No one came walking in the door at 5 pm to give me a break. Single parents and double-shift parents, are you feelin' me? I was in new territory here. None of my friends' husbands traveled. Sometimes I felt like I was stranded on an island, naked and afraid (sounds like an idea for a weird TV show).

This is where I dug deep and went back to the scary place of my mother's wisdom, which I was slowly beginning to recognize as the most remarkable advice anyone would ever give me. How can I make my kids feel special but make less work for myself?

From that thought "Swim Dins" were born. This is a combination of bath time and dinner. I would get my kids' dinner prepared on a plate and take it to the bathroom, where a large body of warm water and pairs of goggles were waiting for them. While the kids swam and played and took their baths, I would feed them their dinner. Voilà! No dinnertime mess to clean up. We didn't have a dog, so it was me that had to sweep up under the kitchen table. I would feed them their food to avoid any sogginess issues. Brilliant. I know. "Swim Dins" became a big hit and created, hands down, some of the best, most memorable evenings I ever spent with my children. Just a reminder: once kids get in the tub they really don't want to get out. Not for any reason. So make sure kids have gone to the bathroom before entering "Swim Din" territory. If not, this could result in a bigger mess to clean up than crumbs under the kitchen table, if you get my drift. The younger they are, the worse the offender. Kate would refuse to get into the tub until Nick went "dumpy doodle" in the potty.

Sometimes I would even do "Backward Swim Dins". We would walk to the bathroom backwards and they would eat dessert first, then sides, then main course. As John Candy said in *Planes, Trains and Automobiles*, "Those are precious moments. They don't come back again."

UNconventional Tip #17

Lie To Your Children

I know most "specialists" would say, "Don't lie to your children." But I say don't be *afraid* to lie to your children. If you really think about it, some of your best memories as parents will come from lying to your children. Take these, for example.

You're going to love your baby brother!

It's completely normal to wear a wig, your sister's swimsuit and smoke fake cigs.

Of course Santa's real.

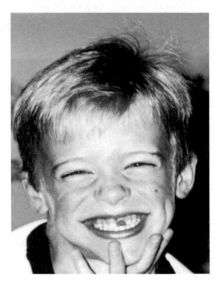

Yes, and the tooth fairy.

Of course someday you'll have a puppy, but in the
meantime enjoy your cousins' dogs.

Don't be silly, of course you will catch a fish.

Yes, you can be a race car driver when you grow up.

Blueberry will be a part of our family for a long, long time.

But my biggest whopper…

Kate, of course I love the Backstreet Boys.

UNconventional Tip #18

Pants Optional

One perfectly good summer day in June of 2000, Kate and Nick were chasing each other down the hallway. We had just come home from early morning swim lessons, and they were running into their rooms to change out of their swimsuits and run outside to play. I heard a thud like someone tripped. I listened and waited for the cry, but nothing came so I ignored it.

A few minutes later Kate finds me in the library. My back is to her and I have no idea she is standing there. (She is my child that just appears out of nowhere and scares the hell out of you.)

Kate: "Mom?"

I turn and look at her.

She is standing with her swimsuit top in her hand, no shirt on and looking like Carrie (reference to an old horror movie for anyone *really* young reading this). Blood is dripping down from her head, down the side of her face, onto her shoulders and chest. She is standing completely still, looking down at her hand that is covered in blood and not saying a word.

Me: "What happened?"

Kate: "I hit my head on that thingy on the wall."

Unfortunately for Kate, she happened to be the exact height of the corners of our thermostat at the time, and she banged her head on it. Who knew thermostats could draw blood?

When things like this happen, I go into this really weird calm mode so as not to upset my kids. (See chapter 28 on "Don't Be Scared Of A Heart Attack".)

Me (super calm and easy breezy): "Well, looks like you got a little cut on your headie bedie. Let's get a washie cloth and take a lookie seekie." (Okay, so I make up words when I'm nervous.)

After applying a cold wash cloth I still can't figure out how deep this cut is. Blood keeps coming. When I was little I cut my forehead trying to climb a fence, and I remember Mom's voice saying, "Even small head wounds bleed like a bitch giving birth to eight puppies." I call our sitter in the neighborhood whose mother happens to be a nurse. They both walk over and within a few minutes Janet confirms it needs stitches.

Kate and I head to the hospital and get in line at the emergency room. While we are waiting to be seen I remember I was supposed to have my first mammogram appointment that afternoon in this very same hospital. I walk over to the check-in desk and ask them to call the hospital's women's center to let them know I am canceling my appointment.

Receptionist is happy to help out and makes the call for me. Receptionist hangs up and says, "Mrs. Steingreaber, they would like you to come upstairs when you are done here with Kate and they will fit you in."

Me: "But there is no way I am going to make that appointment. I should just reschedule."

Receptionist: "They said they will keep the center open for you. We will call them when you are done down here."

I'm listening with half an ear and really have no intention of keeping that appointment. I wasn't looking forward to it anyway. Besides, I was only 35 and none of my friends had ever had one and I didn't know the first thing about it. I had no idea what happens, how it happens or how long it takes. I figured the appointment would take care of itself because the emergency room was packed and there was no way a mammy nurse was going to wait around for me.

Stitches ended up taking a very long time and it's almost six pm when the doctor finishes up. Seeing my kid in pain and covered with blood is starting to take its toll and I'm a little out of it. We are gathering up our stuff from the treatment room when a nurse walks in and says, "Mrs. Steingreaber, I'll walk you to the women's center."

Me (completely forgetting about this appointment after seeing a needle go in and out of my daughter's head): "What? But it's after six o'clock. I'm pretty wiped out."

Nurse: "The radiologic technician is waiting for you but she would like you to hurry."

I am really out of it and too tired to argue. Before I know it, Kate and I are being ushered around the corner, up some stairs and into a dressing room the size of a tiny coat closet. The x-ray tech pops her head in and hands me a dressing gown and says, "When you are ready leave the door open a crack and I'll come get you." News flash: I'm a pretty modest person. Definitely never one to walk around butt naked in a gym locker room. And even if I do tend to lose my pants, sometimes to make a point, I am not one to strip down in front of my children. Kate was sitting on the little bench, still white as a ghost with dried blood caked to her face. I wasn't about to ask her to move. So I get naked (like I do at any other doctor appointment) as fast as I can and quickly grab the paper dressing gown. I pull it over my head. The gown is missing half itself. It only comes to my belly button. I try to pull down on it thinking the rest is tucked up inside but no. Nothing. I am standing there with a paper gown covering my tah tahs but my hot pocket and my badonkadonk are enjoying their freedom. I'm befuddled. It has been a long day already.

Kate: "Mommy, your gina is showing."

Me: "Agreed."

This seems odd. I start looking around for my underwear while opening the door to ask the x-ray tech about the gown. She is waiting by the door, gently grabs my arm and starts to lead me towards the x-ray room. She doesn't blink an eye. She doesn't shout, "For the love of God *PLEASE* put your pants back on!" so I am assuming pants are optional. This *must* be normal protocol. She is in a big hurry and super busy adjusting silver knobs on this giant glass contraption.

Me: "Um…I don't think this is…"

X-ray tech interrupts: "No worries. I'll have you out of here in five minutes."

The rest is a blur. I vaguely remember my breasts being flattened and molded into shapes I thought were impossible. This took my mind off the fact that every time she told me to hold that pose and ran behind me to take the picture she was getting a full-on shot of my ass. My white-as-the-day-I-was-born ass. I was starting to wonder when we progress to that portion of the show that involves my non-covered parts when she says, "We're done. Let me show you back to your room. A radiologist will read the x-rays tomorrow and will call you if you need to come back."

Me: "Wait. So that's it?"

X-ray tech: "That's it."

I walk back to the closet and dress. We get home and I pay the sitter, help Kate get washed (without getting her stitches wet) and let the kids watch a video. I'm exhausted. It's all starting to sink in now. I call Mom.

Me: "Hey, Mom, it's Carol. I just had my first mammogram."

Mom: "Fun times."

Me: "Well, it wasn't too bad really. It only took a few minutes and didn't hurt like some people say. It was just a little uncomfortable."

Mom: "Well, it's a day out of the house and really needs to be done."

A day out of the house? It took five minutes. Does she go for drinks afterwards with friends?

Me: "Yeah, but I was wondering one thing. When you had it done, you didn't take your pants off did you?"

There is silence on the other end of the phone. This is never good. Mom rarely takes time to think about what she is going to say.

Mom: "Oh, Holy Mother of our Lord Jesus. Tell me my college-educated daughter did not remove her pants for her mammogram."

Me: "Um, ha ha, no that would be silly. I mean the gown only comes to below your boobs, right?"

Mom: "Oh, thank you Jesus. For a second there I thought you were going to tell me you were standing naked as the day the good Lord brought you into the world to have a little picture of your breasts taken. That would be dumb. Super dumb."

Of course I'm picturing the x-ray tech out with her co-workers, drinking and laughing herself silly as she tells my story to them. Sigh.

Me: "Anyway, I just called to tell you Kate had to get stitches in her head today."

Mom: "Oh, her first set of stitches. Did you take a picture? We are bringing ice cream over for her." Mom tries to cover up the receiver with her hand but I still get blasted in my ear with, "JERRY! JERRY! There you are! Put on some pants (I now know where I get it from) and pull the car out of the garage. Kate needs ice cream!"

Mom lifts the phone back to her ear, "Did she cry? I bet she didn't. That girl is tough as nails."

Here's my advice (NOT unconventional): DO get a yearly mammogram. They are no big deal. The cool thing? They save lives.

Unconventional advice: DON'T remove your pants. Completely unnecessary but evidently optional.

Here's a picture of Kate proudly displaying her stitches. Upper right corner of picture. Look hard. Look harder. See it now? No? Okay, I will insert an arrow for you.

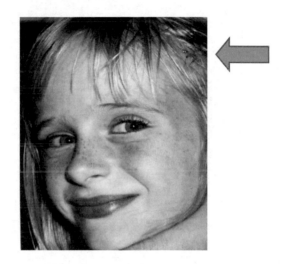

My friend, Ann, went to have her first mammogram a couple of months after me. In her changing room there was a sign that read, "Please Do Not Remove Your Pants."

Ahh…nothing like leaving your mark.

UNconventional Tip #19

Write A Great Christmas Letter

That picture of Nick waiting for Santa reminded me of something important. You must learn how to write a proper Christmas letter. By proper, I mean one that people actually want to read.

Like most people, I love Christmas; it's my favorite season. My favorite part is getting Christmas letters in the mail and writing my own. Writing a good Christmas letter is easy.

However, writing a **_GREAT_** Christmas letter – one that everyone wants to read, that people look for in their mail, that people stop you in the grocery store to ask if you have sent it yet; that has people literally calling and emailing you asking to be put on your Christmas letter mailing list because they were at a mutual friend's house and read your Christmas letter from last year that their friend had kept on their refrigerator, – my friends, **_THAT_** type of Christmas letter takes work and planning.

My shopping, wrapping and mailing of gifts happens the day before Christmas, but writing my Christmas letter starts in January. I start a Word document in January and when funny things happen I write them down. Just a quick sentence to remind me of the incident so that later, when I sit down to create the masterpiece, I have it.

Here is what I DON'T do when I write my Christmas letter:

1. I don't single space. (When you do this people open your letter and freak out and set it aside to be read later when they have two days of nothing to do.)

2.   I don't use the smallest font type known to man. (When people open your letter they see a giant mass of text and have to go get their reading glasses. On the way to get their glasses they realize they don't have two days to sit and read your letter.)

3.   I don't reference my children or husband in every sentence and paragraph. This might come as a surprise to some readers, but no one wants to read paragraph after paragraph of little Jimmy, Sally and Susie's daily life of swim lessons and tee ball games, their reading level in kindergarten and what their favorite binkie, blankie or bedtime story is. (To the millions of you who think this but would never say it out loud... you're welcome.)

Here is what I DO do (love when I can type "do do") when I write my Christmas letter:

1.   Make my Christmas letter funny.

2.   Have a theme and stick to it. People love themes.

3.   Write about things most people don't put in their Christmas letters.

"Like?" you ask.

Joining a nunnery and making whoopee, opening a jockstrap package, eating superglue, empty nest syndrome and using acronyms.

I love my loyal fan base of Christmas letter followers and I try not to disappoint them. To give you a starting point, I am going to combine snippets from six of my past Christmas letters to create one amazing example for you:

Dear Family, Friends and My Faithful Christmas Letter Readers,

Kate, my first child, has left for college. The hardest adjustment is the quiet. Saying that I can whisper to myself in the house and hear an echo is an understatement. It's so quiet I keep expecting to see cloistered nuns walking around the living room. Nick, my 16-year-old, is not a big communicator. Grunts and a head nod pass as a month's worth of communication. (Anyone with a teenage boy – can I get an Amen?) And with Paul traveling every week, I actually feel like a cloistered nun! Good news! Paul and I just returned from celebrating our wedding anniversary in Scottsdale, Arizona, where we golfed every day and Paul reminded me every night that I am not a cloistered nun.

Paul got some new jockstraps. He needed help opening them up. They were packaged in this crazy, rigid, industrial plastic clamshell container where you have to get your heavy-duty scissors out and you try to cut it but you need both hands on the scissors to get the scissors to work and still only get a small slice started. Then, the part of the plastic you were actually able to cut starts to cut your hand because it's so sharp. Eventually, you have one side cut and you think you have opened the package far enough, so you try to pull it apart but your knuckles get all bloodied trying to pry the package open. I tried sticking my hand inside the package to retrieve the (insert your item here – curling iron, flashlight, gaming equipment, electronics); ours, of course, was jockstraps. Paul put on his winter snow-shoveling gloves and tried to pull the package apart but I finally got it opened by beating it with a hammer and then using the prongs on the hammer to pull it apart. I got a couple of bloodied knuckles and sliced fingers in that adventure. Strap on your seatbelt. Use your cushion as a floatation device. We are just getting started, kids!

Not all of my adventures involved blood. Some were a grueling trial of mental toughness and head-scratching. One day I noticed my mom's dentures were starting to slip out of her mouth every time she spoke. So I asked her about it and she showed me where a hole had developed in her dentures. Next time I saw her I asked her about the hole and suggested seeing a dentist, and she said Dad had plugged the hole with superglue. Hmmm. I said, "Hey, Mom? Superglue isn't for human consumption." She informed me she wasn't eating it. She said it worked great for Dad's front tooth that broke off when he was eating some peanut brittle.

Empty Nest is a breeze. My last child has left to fly planes and run track at Utah State. At first, Paul and I were sad. Then with some really good therapy (talks in front of the fire) and GREAT wine we saw what REALLY lay in front of us…Nick not asking us for any more money, Nick not borrowing our gas card, Nick not drinking the last of the water and leaving the empty jug in the refrigerator, Nick not putting his laundry in the wash and leaving it there for weeks, Nick not putting the cracker box back in the cupboard with just ONE cracker in it so he won't have to recycle the box…This could go on and on but I feel confident you get the point. Needless to say, Paul and I are embracing the Empty Nest Syndrome.

Steingreabers only speak in acronyms now. Paul still enjoys his job as Regional VP for VOYA Financial™. He got his CIMA certification but has to go to IMCA meetings to keep it current. BTW, we are now on DST and FYI we do enjoy some R&R and a good BLT and PB&J every now and again. When Paul plays golf, he does love his GIRs. I love a good acronym.

And we love you all. Have a blessed Christmas and New Year! – The Steingreabers.

If you follow this advice I know you can have a loyal fan base of Christmas letter followers, and fewer people will toss your letter in their fireplace before reading it.

UNconventional Tip #20

Use Visual Aids When Making Points To Your Kids

When my daughter needed some extra parental help I could usually just sit her down and explain that what she did was wrong, and why. Or, if she had a crazy idea that didn't make any sense, I could walk her through her idea from beginning to dead end, and that would be sufficient.

With my son, however, actions spoke louder than words (see chapter 15, "Play Plumber"). He is a visual learner. He must see with his own eyes that what he is doing/saying/thinking makes no sense.

Like most boys, my son was obsessed with sports. Baseball, soccer, football – you name it – he knew all the players and their stats. Nick and his dad would pore over every issue of Sports Illustrated together. Of course, every year included the SI Swimsuit edition. If Paul got the mail first, he was able to peruse this edition for a bit before he recycled it. If I happened to get the mail first the day the SI Swimsuit edition came out, I would drop it right in the recycle bin. Our little system took a turn one year when Nick got home before me and had brought in the mail (because he had heard from his friends "THE" magazine had arrived). He was a freshman in high school at the time. He was standing at the kitchen counter perusing it when I walked in.

Again, going back to my parents' mantra that "No topic is off the table", I dove right in.

Me: "Nicholas, that magazine is pornography. Throw it in the recycling bin."

Nick: "Mom" – he was starting to make a point, but got distracted by half-naked women.

I knew I needed to strike while he was dazed and disarmed. Once again I relied on my UTI (Unconventional Thinking Initiative).

Me: "Hey, my little numb nut, if you can give me one good reason why you should be looking through that magazine, you can have it." Nick looked at me completely dumbfounded. Here was his one chance.

Nick: "Mom, you get a new swimsuit every summer. You can use this mag to pick one out."

I don't think I have ever laughed so hard inside while keeping a straight face on the outside. But here was *my* one chance to nip (no pun intended) this in the bud.

Me: "Okay, Nick. I am going to find my new swimsuit in here and when I do, I will give the magazine back to you."

Nick, convinced he had this one in the bag, quickly handed it over.

I perused. It didn't take long. I found the perfect swimsuit. Then I found a picture of myself in our family photo album. I cut out a picture of my head and glued it onto a woman (this was my version of scrap bookin') who was using a Hawaiian Lei as her swimsuit top.

Me: "Nick! Lookie here. Found one. Great idea, by the way. This mag is awesome. I don't know why I didn't think of this before. Forget Land's End. I'm not buying another swimsuit from that catalog. I'm sure your friends won't mind seeing me in this at the pool this summer. What happens when the flowers on the Lei dry up? Hmmm… I don't know what I am gonna do for bottoms, though? Any ideas? She didn't have any on in this picture."

Over the years when we get the SI Swimsuit edition, I send Nick pictures of me with the new swimsuits I have chosen. This year I bought two. Wildflowers and ripped fishing nets. Who knew these would make amazing swimsuits?

UNconventional Tip #21

Only On The Bed

With Paul traveling every week and me staying home with the kids, we quickly discovered our marriage was very "unique" (extremely challenging) and needed special attention if we were going to last till death do us part.

The only time we would have together would be the weekends. Naturally, Paul would want to spend morning till night with the kids since he hadn't been with them. This left from about 10:00 pm till we passed out at 10:15 pm for "us" time.

As a result, our time for making whoopee, bumping uglies, the two-back monster, knocking boots, slap and tickle, mattress dancing, hanky panky, getting busy, threading the needle or burying the bone was limited.

We decided that a trip once a year, just the two of us, was a must. It would be like a marriage retreat but instead of sleeping on an air mattress in a gymnasium with complete strangers, we would stay in a resort, have fresh, clean sheets every day and room service. We would attempt conversation without interruption and enjoy sleeping in. We also used these trips to discover that 10:05-10:15 pm was not the only time we could thread the needle.

Of course leaving for vacation and packing off two little children was daunting. We would drive the kids to Paul's parents' house for the week (a two-hour drive). It would take hours to unload the van and get the kids moved into Gammy and Gampy's house. The van would be packed to the rafters with toys, a play pen, a baby gym, and a bath ring for Kate, a baby bath tub for Nick, two car seats and a stroller. Not to mention baby formula, bottles, burp rags, bibs, diapers, seven days of clothing for two kids, sleepers and a high chair. Then, we would still have our two-hour drive to the Cedar Rapids airport.

By the time Paul and I got to the airport, we would be exhausted. We would agree emphatically we were never going through all this work again and then proceed to pass out on the plane. But after a week together, all the work would be a distant memory (like childbirth) and we would do it all over again a year later.

During our annual honeymoon getaway, I would really pour on the sex appeal: shower daily, wash and dry my hair, put on makeup and wear something other than sweats. No baseball cap and hair in a ponytail. No sir. I would step it up to new levels. I would also insist Paul and I thread the needle somewhere other than the bed. I would start in, "Life's too short. We need to mix it up." Yada yada yada.

This never went over well. Paul likes it traditional, maybe a nightlight on but most certainly on the bed. I knew if we were to keep it fresh it would become important for me to help him break this habit.

One year, at a hotel in Scottsdale, there was a desk that looked like it could be my answer. Paul was already pulling back the comforter and closing the curtains. It was two in the afternoon.

Me: "Hey, lookie here big fella."

I have removed all lamps and cords and writing instruments from the desk and am partially sitting on it. Naked.

Paul: "What are you doing on the desk?"

Me: "Well, I thought we could make whoopee on it."

Paul says, visibly turned on but his Mr. Safety doppelganger kicking in, "I don't think that is a good idea. What if we break it?"

Realizing he was actually considering it, I started throwing caution to the wind.

Me: "We're not going to break it. Let's just start here and then we can move to the bed."

That did it. We were off and running. I had high hopes of completing the entire transaction on this desk. It would be a new chapter in our lives. I was envisioning waterfalls, the ocean, even the back seat of our car. We were a good thirty minutes into it when we hear a weird sound. Next thing I know the table is breaking and I am falling backwards through the air. Paul grabs me and lifts me away just as the table breaks but before my entire back and bare ass land in a huge pile. Of broken glass. Big chunks of jagged shards. Did I mention the desk was made of glass?

Okay, that wasn't my best idea but I had good intentions. Paul saved my life that day. Did that episode reinforce his Mr. Safety tendencies? Yes. I had definitely lost ground in that area. Needless to say, we are back to the bed. Safety first.

Funny thing though, when you have a bad idea and someone saves your life, they don't let you forget it. Throughout the course of a year, that particular moment tends to be revisited by Paul multiple times, especially if I happen to be throwing caution to the wind, like when I ride no-handed on my 10-speed.

So how do you stop someone from bringing up the fact they saved your life? You even the score.

About two years after the glass table episode, we found ourselves at a TGI Fridays. Not a favorite of mine but Paul was a big fan. We sit down and he orders the French onion soup as an appetizer. Within minutes his soup arrives. I have a crayon in my hand and start to draw the hangman game on the paper tablecloth (classy). My word is croquet. No double letters and no chance he'll guess the letter q before he's hung. I draw seven spaces _ _ _ _ _ _ _. I'm switching crayon colors when Paul starts pounding on the table. I look up and realize he is choking on the mozzarella cheese that comes melted on top of the soup. I jump out of my chair and run around the table. I perform the Heimlich. Cheese comes up! Not really flying out of his mouth, like you see in the videos, but close. Bam! We're even.

We can go years and years without Paul bringing up the glass table now. Plus, I never have to go to another TGI Fridays ever again. It was a win-win for me.

UNconventional Tip #22

Embarrass Your Kids

I love being silly. I love being a kid when I can get away with it. Halloween is the best holiday for showing your kids that you are never too old for fun. I feel bad for those kids that think they are too cool for certain things.

Don't be afraid to embarrass your kids. Be silly. Have fun. You are sending your children two important messages: You don't care what others think, and life is too short to miss out on fun no matter what your age. There were times I had my kids' voices telling me in one ear that I am embarrassing them but in my other ear I would hear my parents' voices once again reminding me, "Don't take life so seriously! Tomorrow isn't promised!" One thing I did know, the voices needed to stop so I could avoid meds down the road.

Even before I had kids, I dressed up as Snow White. I have trick or treated with my kids while wearing the costume and still to this day I pass out candy as Snow White. The little children that come to my door are surprised when I open it and Snow White appears. One year a group of kids were on my doorstep ringing my bell. I had passed out the candy and all had dispersed but one little girl in a princess costume. She motioned for me with her finger to come close to listen to her. I crouched down to hear her. She whispered in my ear, "Please don't eat the apple."

Once, when Paul happened to be in town on Halloween, he asked me, "Hey, Snow White, where are your dwarfs?" I replied, "Under my dress, of course," and gave him a look like this:

Even my son borrowed my Snow White costume one Halloween. Once again, the issue of dressing in women's clothing reared its head, but Nick loves a good laugh as much as me so I let him use it.

Another Halloween my mom was having some health issues, and I was a little bit down and wasn't up to wearing my costume to pass out candy. Nick, a high school junior at the time, who was only conversing with me by using grunting sounds, stopped his world and asked why wasn't I dressed in my SW costume to pass out candy. I told him I wasn't up for it and he berated me into putting it on. "Kids are counting on you, Mom! They look forward to seeing you in it. What's the matter with you? Get your head in the game! Be a team player! It's Halloween!"

At that very moment I knew I had done something right by ignoring all the years when my kids were embarrassed by me.

Another bonus: With all the costume craziness over the years I have actually instilled a love of Halloween in them.

Kate is a senior in college and still dresses up every Halloween. Sophomore year she went as one of the Kick Ass characters. She was Red Mist (on left), Caleb was Kick Ass and Kayla Hit Girl.

Junior year her and her roomies, Kayla and Chelsea, were loofahs.

This year lots of her friends dressed as multiple characters of Johnny Depp.

Kate was Edward Scissorhands. Amazing!

UNconventional Tip #23

Have A Tradition Nobody Else Understands

When raising my kids, every now and again I would listen to the "experts". I never used the word stupid or dumb-dumb (out loud). I didn't have to. When my kids were being stupid, I called them something they would come to understand meant the same thing.

Jim.

My brother, Marty, started this tradition in our family. He was a huge Star Trek fan and loved Dr. Bones. There was an episode where Captain Kirk was asking Bones to do something extraordinary. Bones yells, "Damnit Jim! I'm just a country doctor." So our family adopted this line. It was used thousands of times while I was growing up.

Dad: "Marty, climb up onto the roof and clean out all the gutters and replace some shingles for me."

Marty: "Damnit Jim! I'm just a country doctor!"

Mom: "Carol, make 800 pounds of oatmeal chocolate chip cookies for the Reilly Reunion."

Me: "Damnit Jim! I'm just a country doctor!"

You get the picture.

Somewhere along the way the line got shortened to Jim. Just Jim. And then used in multiple ways and references, ultimately meaning dumb-dumb.

Of course my kids didn't understand for many, many years why I called them Jim. They would laugh and say, "Mommy! You silly! You forgot my name!"

When my son had a piece of gum in his mouth and was lying on the living room floor, he got to laughing and the gum got stuck in his windpipe. Fortunately, I managed to do a makeshift Heimlich and the gum came flying out like a rocket.

Me: "JIM! What are you doing lying down with gum in your mouth?"

Nick suddenly becomes very still, I'm assuming with the realization he could have choked to death had I not been here. And what does he say? "Mom, you just forgot my name. AGAIN!"

And so it started.

"Jim, yes you have to repay a loan from a bank. Just because you 'qualify' for the loan doesn't mean you WIN it."

"Jim, I'm not dropping you off a block away. Your friends know I exist."

"Jim, grab a coat. It's ten below outside. Wind chill is thirty below." Just an FYI, it really does get that cold here in the Midwest. I wish I was exaggerating.

"Jim, where are the eggs I sent you to the store for? There are only Funyons, Gatorade and a movie rental in this bag."

Nick: "Oh…I forgot." (I love that my kids actually answer to the name Jim.)

Me: "Jimmy! Don't make me start calling you Ifer."

UNconventional Tip #24

Enjoy Your Period

Like my parents taught me, no topic is ever off the table. However, I never thought I would say this…I miss Aunt Flo.

Remember when Aunt Flo would come to visit at the absolute worst possible times? A friend would ask to use your last tampon in your jumbo box. What's the worst that could happen? You'll go to Target tomorrow, right? So you hand over the tampon. An hour later…BAM! Cramps and ruined underwear. And a trip to Target with toilet paper stuffed into your hooch.

I have the BEST friends. No topic is off the table with them. Regularly, a friend would happily announce at a GNO (girl's night out), "I have my period! I don't have to have sex tonight!" You'd think they'd won the lottery.

Another would say, "Gawd, I asked for a back rub last night. Just a back rub. But no. The hands eventually make their way around to my boobs. I even did the blockade. You know? Stiff arms down to my side to block the invasion. Just one time I would like a back rub that starts as a back rub and ends a back rub."

Having my period never worked with Paul. Believe me, I tried.

We would climb into bed and he would test the waters. Soft rubbing and cuddling. Kind words whispered in my ear. I immediately would nip this in the bud to save valuable sleep time.

Me: "Honey, I have my period."

Paul: "Sweetness, your body is like an amusement park. Just because the main ride is under repair, doesn't mean the entire park is closed down. There are still lots of fun things to see and do."

So when Aunt Flo completely left the building, I was giddy at first. About six months went by without missing Aunt Flo one iota. I loved not buying tampons. And, not worrying about dying of toxic shock syndrome when I would try to count up how many hours I had left my tampon in.

But then, I heard a knock on my door. It was Aunt Flo's bitter nemesis, Menopause. She was like Mary Poppins' evil stepsister. Her big carpet bag held a lot of things but nothing fun like a fringed lamp or an umbrella with a talking parrot. Oh no. Meno reached into her bag and pulled out about 20 pounds of fat that she immediately tied around my waist. She pulled out a colorful spritz bottle and sprayed a mist of confusion and fog into the air that my brain soaked up like a sponge. Then, when I wasn't looking, Meno stole my short term memory and hid it. Last but not least, she pulled out a fan and instantly zapped all the moisture of out my body to the point where people mistook my legs for crocodiles.

Actually, do you remember the Lubriderm lotion commercial where the woman is laying on a white chaise lounge and the alligator saunters past? That's me. The alligator. I auditioned for that part and got it after Menopause moved in with me.

To tell you the truth, I rarely ever talk about Menopause. It is kind of pointless because even when you try to complain about Menopause, there is always some woman who has it worse than you. I call her the Meno Topper. She sweats more than you. Sleeps less than you. Cries more randomly than you. Her tears are bigger than yours. It just goes on and on. So I prefer to speak about it as little as possible. Most of my friends have yet to experience Meno's full force. And I don't want to rob them of the entire journey so the less I say the better. I just tell them to enjoy their period and they look at me like I am crazy.

Red wine drinkers beware. Red wine makes hot flashes worse. The way I see it, you have two options. You can stop drinking red wine during menopause. Or, you can drink red wine naked in front of a fan. Obviously, there is only one clear choice. You can get a good fan for about twenty bucks.

UNconventional Tip #25

Make Friends With An Only Child

When it comes to friends, Paul has one-upped me. He has an only child as a best friend.

Of course his name is Paul. Paul and Paul have been friends since childhood. It got better when Paul and his wife, Debbie, moved to Des Moines, Iowa, when Paul and I were still living there.

It was always complicated when Debbie and I would be talking about our husbands. Deb would say, "Paul is so sweet, Carol."

Me: "What did he do now?"

Debbie: "He stopped by after work to help with something in the garage."

Me: "What? How does that make him sweet? It's his house."

Debbie: "No, your Paul. Your Paul stopped by here after work."

Me: "My Paul stopped by after work? What was your Paul doing?"

Debbie: "My Paul needed his help with something in the garage."

Me: "Oh. Gotcha."

So to save valuable time we always go by "your Paul or my Paul" when conversing.

Of course, Debbie and Paul made it more difficult by naming their son, Paul. Conversations became a Laurel and Hardy Who's On First game.

We got in on the act by naming our son Nicholas Paul, naturally.

After sharing years of your lives with great friends you develop tag lines. One evening after dinner and shenanigans, Debbie and her Paul were leaving our apartment. Her Paul had been very gassy that evening so I said to Debbie on the way out, "Good luck with *that* on the drive home." Her Paul started yelling, "GOOD LUCK TO YA!" at the top of his lungs and waking all inhabitants of West Des Moines, Iowa.

As a consequence to that, now, every time we have seen each other and are ending the visit, we keep yelling, "GOOD LUCK TO YA!" until we have driven away and can't hear the other family any longer. Even our kids get into it yelling out the car windows.

I will have to admit it took me some time to warm up to Paul (Debbie's Paul). There was something about him I couldn't quite put my finger on. Our friendship included a lot of bantering, teasing, and trying to outsmart each other. I had never met anyone like him before. He had a certain air about him. He was an enigma to me. I mean, here we were, early twenties, but he spoke intelligently with parents and other adults, like it came naturally to him. He had a confidence I had never seen before. It seemed like whatever Debbie's Paul wanted he got, just by asking for it. Not to mention that his big, booming voice commanded your attention from the moment he walked into a room.

One day I said to my Paul, "I don't mean to be mean, but I think Debbie's Paul is a bit spoiled." I whispered *spoiled* like it was a dirty word. Then I added in a smug, know-it-all voice, "He's obviously the baby of his family."

My Paul: "You're wrong. He's an only child."

Me: "WHAT?"

Okay, first I had to realize I was actually wrong. It had been a few years so that took some getting used to.

But now a bigger insight awaited me.

I had never met a man who was an only (gasp!) child before.

I had no idea I was being forced into a relationship with a whole different species. This made sense to me now. No wonder he was so different from me. Debbie's Paul had never been told, "Just wait a minute! I'm helping your brother get the stick out of his eye." Debbie's Paul had probably never even been to a garage sale, never wore hand-me-downs or had to assume ownership of used stereo equipment. And (going to go out on a limb here) he probably had his own bedroom and when he used the bathroom, probably got to close the door. His mom never said, "Your sisters just ate the last piece of pie. You can lick the plate if you want."

All of my good friends growing up had siblings. Lots of them. We were cut from the same cloth. You could pick up any one of us and insert us into another large family and it would be days before the parents realized they had another kid hanging around.

Let's be honest. It came down to this. How could I trust someone who never had to share?

But then, one morning, the good Lord (who has a mean sense of humor), put me in a position to learn a valuable lesson. Before I knew it, Debbie's Paul made it perfectly clear to me the most amazing quality of an only child.

I had just had Kate and was home on maternity leave. My Paul was out of town. I had diarrhea (diarrhea where I couldn't get off the toilet for more than a minute diarrhea).

I needed help. I decided I had to make a run for it. I took a wad of TP, covered my trap door and ran hunched over into the bedroom to grab the phone. I ran back to the toilet. I regrouped and quickly dialed Debbie.

Me: "Hey, Deb, it's Carol. My Paul's out of town. Is there any way you could run me over some meds that will help me get off the shitter? I have nothing in my medicine cabinet but Preparation H and disposable nursing pads."

Debbie: "That would be a job for Imodium A-D." (I am assuming the A-D stands for About to Die.)

Me: "I'm not picky. I'll use whatever you have."

Debbie: "Sorry, but I can't help you right now. I'll call my Paul."

Click.

Me: "No! Deb?" Buzzing noise.

What Deb doesn't know is that I am half naked on the upstairs toilet. I have removed my underwear and jeans (once again pantless) so as to keep my body temperature from making me burst into flames. Kate's in the car carrier next to me on the bathroom floor. She is starting to let it be known that she can't handle much more of the stench that keeps creeping up her nostrils. I can tell you that I have maybe cried about five times in my life. This was one of those times. I started crying and couldn't stop.

Phone rings.

Debbie: "My Paul's on his way." Click.

This situation was bad and was about to get a lot worse and extremely embarrassing. About twenty minutes later I hear the front door open and close. Debbie's Paul in his booming voice starts yelling for me.

Me: "Paul! I'm upstairs (gulp and catch my breath because I am still crying) in the bathroom!"

I hear Paul going through my cupboards in my kitchen and then the water running. He comes upstairs. The door is open. He hands me the grocery bag and puts down the glass of water on the sink. He picks up Kate and turns and goes downstairs.

That's it.

No harassing comments. No teasing me about how I look (and smell) like shit. No irritation that he had to leave work. No comment about my lower extremities being pale, hairy (I had yet to shave off the nine months of pregnancy hair on my legs) and without pants.

I dry my tears. Take a couple of pills. Within about forty-five minutes my underwear and jeans are back on and I am slowly walking downstairs, clenching my butt cheeks and not trusting a fart. Debbie's Paul is sitting on the couch in the living room with Kate on his lap.

Me: "I don't know what to say. I think that might be the nicest thing anyone has ever done for me. I have brothers that wouldn't have been that nice. Oh, sure, they would have done it but I would never hear the end of it. I can't thank you enough."

Debbie's Paul: "Glad you're starting to feel better. It's no fun taking care of kids when you don't feel good." He hands me Kate, ruffles the hair on my head like I'm twelve and yells, "Good luck to ya!" as he's walking out the door.

Loyalty.

That's what I couldn't put my finger on. It snuck up on me and smacked me in the face. Debbie's Paul is the most fiercely loyal friend my Paul has ever had. Debbie's Paul never had a sibling. His best friend *is* his brother. There is ***nothing*** that Debbie's Paul won't do for his best friend and his family. He has shown that same loyalty to me and my kids over and over throughout the years. Even though we live thousands of miles apart now, when we talk on the phone, it's just like we are back in West Des Moines, reliving our shenanigans in the skywalks of downtown Des Moines.

Here's Debbie's Paul dancing with my Paul's sister, Kristin, at our wedding. Why? Because that is what best friends do. GOOD LUCK TO YA!

UNconventional Tip #26

Hit The APS With A Friend

Attention all women! Nourish your gal pals, BFFs, Chiquitas, road hoes and homies. I know I have already mentioned it, but I will say it again. I have GREAT friends. Each and every one of my friends looks at life completely differently compared to other people. I love that about them and I admire them for it. And like my wise friend Ann once told me, if you are truly lucky and blessed, there comes a time in your life where you say, "Yeah, I'm not interviewing for new friends."

Friends don't become great friends and stay great friends by accident. It's easy to maintain your friendships during your high school and college years. Even after you get married, staying in touch with your friends or making new friends is pretty simple. But once you have kids, months can go by before you realize you haven't A) showered or B) gotten together with a friend.

I have to be the luckiest woman in the world. I have a circle of friends that the Justice League would envy. They are the most amazing and eclectic group of women. I have a woman in my life that I have known since second grade. I have some high school friends that I couldn't possibly live without. I have friends in my life that I met through my kids, through other friends and through my work. Plus, my girlfriends from Loras College (we call ourselves "The Losers" because we studied so much – inserted for Kate and Nick's benefit) try to get together once a year. When we see each other we put an "L" to our forehead as a sign of our solidarity.

Catherine, my second-grade buddy, is like a sister. I see her at least twice a week for our workout and therapy sessions. We can usually solve all the problems of the world in an hour and a half (plus our own). We have saved millions of dollars on counselors by telling each other what we are doing wrong and how to proceed through life and marriage.

I love how Catherine looks at life. She strips it down to the bare bones. She keeps it simple and uncomplicated. She sees a solution, then tweaks it and you find yourself saying, "Why didn't I think of that?"

Catherine: "I'm having trouble getting my three kids dressed in the morning. It's taking too long for them to pick out their clothes. I've been late for work twice this week."

Me: "Have them lay their clothes out the night before." I'm a genius, right?

Next day.

Me: "How did the morning go? Did you get to work on time?"

Catherine: "Problem solved. Loved your idea. HUGE time saver and I have less laundry to do."

I was scared to ask.

Me: "Why less laundry?"

Catherine: "I have my kids sleep in their school clothes. Everyone's happy. Kids wake up dressed. I get to work on time. Bam! Someday we should write a book."

Here's Catherine and I on our Confirmation day. We would learn beneficial lessons from this photo later in life, like the value of hair care products. I was still using Tide thanks to my dad. But we were rocking the knee-highs and the saints' names. Catherine at least had some style, thanks to that scarf.

This may have been the last time I wore a dress. Pretty sure I still have those barrettes.

In the fall of 2004 I met a new friend, Lisa. Our boys were in the same grade. We hit it off right away. It truly was like we had known each other our entire lives.

We were a few months into our friendship when I get this call.

Lisa: "Hey, can you meet me at the Adult Porn Shop?"

In my mind: Sure, right after I drop my youngest off at vacation bible school and pick up some groceries you crazy, Jazzercise nut-job.

Me: "Um…I think you have the wrong number."

Lisa: "Carol, it's Lisa. I need to go to the APS and you are the only person I know who will go with me."

Me: "Excuse me a minute while I put the phone down because I am more than a little insulted."

Lisa: "Why would you be insulted? This is the highest form of compliment I could possibly give a friend."

Now at this point I realize that perhaps I may have jumped into this particular friendship a little too fast. Lisa is obviously delusional.

Me: "I was actually just on my way to church when you called."

Lisa: "Stop it. Don't you see? You have the best sense of humor. You have the confidence to pull this off. You will make this fun. I am dreading it. My sister is getting married and I am in charge of the bachelorette party. Damn her for getting married so late in my life. I'm already a mom with four kids! I'm too old to be walking into a porn shop without it looking creepy."

Me: "I don't think there is an age restriction on that."

Lisa: "I am leaving right now. Meet me there."

Me: "Lisa, it's 1:30 in the afternoon. We have stickers on the back of our car windows with our kids' school emblems on them. We are going to have to be smart about this. We can't have people see our cars parked in the lot."

Lisa: "Good point."

Me: "We'll ride together and back your van right up to the front of the building. People driving by will only see the van from the side."

Lisa: "Makes sense. Every mother in this city has a van just like mine. No one will know it's me. I just want plates, napkins, cups and straws. It shouldn't take too long. I will even have my check written out except the amount so checkout will go fast."

Me: "JIM! You are not writing a check at an adult porn shop. We will stop at the bank on our way and get you some cash."

Lisa: "Perfect! Good thinking! See, this is why I called you. You can think rationally about these things. It means a lot to me you doing this. I couldn't do it by myself."

Me: "Well, I actually do feel a *little* honored that you called me. And when Paul asks me what I did today I'll actually have something interesting to report. Now let's go get you some penis straws."

UNconventional Tip #27

Read Between The Wines

In 2004, my dear friend, Joyce, asked me if I wanted to join a book club she was in. Here I was with a degree in English Literature and another degree in Writing, and I had never been in a book club. I was intrigued, so I said I would give it a test run. If you've never been in a book club I suggest you join one. If nothing else, at least you know that once a month someone is going to pour you a glass of yummy wine and ask your opinion on something.

I don't know how many of you readers are part of a book club, but what I *do* know is there is no way you are part of a book club like mine.

My book club is no-nonsense. We rip a book apart like the sharks on Shark Week rip apart a seal. No writer should ever consider publishing a book until our book club has had a chance to read it. We are like Oprah. Our critique could turn your book into a bestseller, or might make you collapse into a fetal position and cry like a baby yelling, "Make it stop!"

When these women are all gathered under one roof it rivals any Geneva Convention in the history of the world. I know you think I'm exaggerating but I'm not. These women are some of the most intelligent, well-spoken, well-read women on the face of the planet. I have great respect for each and every one of them. Just by being in the same room with these ladies I can feel new brain cells multiplying. Bill Gates and President Obama have no idea of the talent that sits beneath a single roof once a month, because if they did they would find a way to harness it (with the exception of myself, of course; I am basically used for comic relief).

Saying our book club is organized is a massive understatement. We voted on a name for our book club, "Reading Between the Wines", and we have a secretary, Joyce, who keeps a list of all the books we have read and the authors, and which one of us chose the book (used to ridicule the unsuspecting member later if the book was awful).

Plus, we even have a system where a different person chooses the book each month. When it's your turn to choose and announce the Book of the Month, you also include vital information such as how many copies the library has, how many e-books and large print books are available, how many copies are checked out and the wait list time, how many copies Half Price Books has and if Barnes and Noble even carries it. I spent about the same amount of time researching my college thesis.

If we are reading one Oprah book after another (these are books Oprah recommends and they always leave you exhausted, with an empty box of Kleenex by your night stand and troubled for weeks) I break the flow and make the ladies read, "Are You There Vodka? It's Me, Chelsea" by

Chelsea Handler, or "Me Talk Pretty One Day" by David Sedaris.

The day after book club, Joyce even sends out an email to all of the members summarizing in her unique, witty way, what was discussed at book club and the title and author of the next book we will be reading. This is very important because by the end of the night my mind is mush. Book club for me is like cramming for a final – too many smart things coming at me at once.

This book club is a well-oiled machine and I feel honored to be a part of it. But before we sit down to discuss a book, we have social hour. These ladies can't dumb it down. Even social hour can get intense. Here's a taste of a typical social hour conversation (a teensy bit exaggerated but you get the idea).

Joyce: "Well, ladies, we are closer to solving the escalation of unrest in the Ukraine, despite Obama and Putin."

Pam: "I am happy to pass along the positive economic reports of U.S. retailers shaking off the winter blahs. Let's see if we can make Eddie Bauer turn a profit this year. Be sure and check out our new store at Lindale Mall."

Jill: "Jody, Kristi, Carol (not me, the other one) and I have solved the security breaches at Target and on eBay." (This Carol is a music teacher whose entire family is adorable and sings like angels. Every one – all six – can sing. Think Von Trapp.)

Mary: "Maria and I think we might have a cure for Ebola."

How I haven't been kicked out of this book club I'll never know. When my book gets published I have a feeling this is how that particular social hour conversation might go…

Me: "Hey Wine-ers. I thought I would read a little from my book since none of you have had a chance to read it yet what with solving all the world's problems, taking care of your amazing families, working your jobs and volunteering."

All Wine-ers: "We've tried but the library only has one copy and it is always checked out."

Me: "Um…you could buy my book."

Complete silence.

Me: "Has no one bought my book? I've been in book club with you for *TEN* years! You'd think someone would buy my book! It's **BOOK** club! *I. WROTE. A. BOOK*!"

Joyce: "Carol, calm down. I think now would be a good time to kick Carol out of book club. All in favor say Aye!"

And it is the quiet ones that are ruthless. We read a book once by a local author we had almost asked to come to our book club. The host that month was really glad she didn't, as none of us liked the book. The book club was a bloodbath. Maria hadn't said much the entire night. She was keeping it all bottled up. Our host asked Maria her opinion.

Maria takes a moment to gather her thoughts, takes a sip of wine and then says, "Well, if this book would have been written by another writer and would have been about something completely different, I think I would have liked it." Ouch.

UNconventional Tip #28

Don't Be Scared Of A Heart Attack

In 2006, both of my kids were in middle school, Kate in eighth grade and Nick in sixth. I was starting to get antsy. The days seemed long and my creativity was screaming at me to let it out. So I went in search of the perfect job. This job would have to allow me to take my kids to school, work my job, and leave early enough to run errands and still be able to pick my kids up from school. Did a job like this even exist?

I dug out my old resume. Wow. A big chunk of my life was missing from 1993 to 2006. How do I make being a stay-at-home mom sound like the best job in the world?

Homemaker from April 1993 to Present.

- These past thirteen years I've been dealing in futures (a.k.a. raising my children).
- In my free time I made lots of margaritas, ate chips and salsa and had as many GNOs as humanly possible. If you hire me, I will give you my fabulous margarita recipe my good friend, Mary, gave me.
- Will give you a signed autographed copy of my book that I am going to write (someday).

Okay, sounded good.

Timing is everything. Within three months I had my dream job.

I was two weeks into my dream job when I was forced into making this phone call from the hospital to my boss...

Me: "Good morning, Mike. Hey, I won't be coming into work today because I think I'm going to have surgery. No, no didn't see this coming. Will keep you posted. Have a good day."

Click. Not a phone call I wanted to make but *kind* of worth it.

Let's back up the truck.

The night before, we were all sitting down to dinner when all of a sudden I felt like I was having a heart attack. It felt like there was a huge rubber band squeezed tight around my body underneath my breast bone. It hurt to breathe. I quickly got up from the table and went back to my bedroom because I didn't want to upset the kids (the weird workings of a mom's mind). Paul knew something was wrong and followed me.

Me: "Something is weird. I feel like I am having a heart attack but I know in my brain I am not."

Paul: "Your brain isn't your strong suit. I am going to call the ambulance."

Me: "No! I don't want to upset the kids."

Paul: "Um…you dying would upset the kids."

Me: "Okay. The pain is already going away. I'm feeling better. Do not call an ambulance. I am fine. I am just going to rest on the couch in the living room for a while."

I lay down and I remember Paul saying something about not falling asleep and then I don't remember anything after that. The next thing I know I'm awake, sitting up on the couch looking up at four male firefighters, two male police officers and two EMT people (one man and one woman).

Me: "Oh my God, this is my fantasy come true. One at a time please, just remove your shirts and dance a little. Hip gyration welcomed but not mandatory. Um, not you, Miss, although your coworker might like that."

Firefighter: "Mrs. Steingreaber, we need to check your vitals."

Me: "No no. No talking. There is no talking in my fantasy."

Vitals taken, albeit roughly.

EMT: "You seem very alert. Even cracking jokes. Your vitals are registering normal. I would still recommend that we transport you to the hospital for further testing."

Me: "Not necessary."

Paul: "Not an option. You're going in the ambulance and I will follow in about a half hour. Your parents are on their way over to be with the kids."

A stretcher was produced from thin air, and before I knew it I was strapped down on the bed heading out the door. Disappointment set in when I realized none of the firefighters would jump onto my bed and go for a quick ride with me out to the waiting ambulance. Would have loved to wrap up and put a bow on my entire fantasy by saying, "I was in bed with a firefighter."

Turns out gallbladder flare-ups mimic heart attack symptoms. My gallbladder had to be removed. That was *not* a fantasy.

UNconventional Tip #29

Be Superior At Relaxing

I have the best job. I brag to my friends about how great my job is. My girlfriends, Ann and Mary, will see my bosses out at social events and try to take my job from me. They'll talk smack about me, and then write their resumes on cocktail napkins and hand them to Mike and Kourtné (MK).

I work for a husband-and-wife chiropractic team. Mike let me decide on my title, since this was a new position in their clinic. I call myself a Marketing Director. Now this is a little bit of a stretch, because technically you should probably work fulltime to have such a fancy title and all, but nonetheless I quickly had it printed on things before Mike could change his mind.

Our working relationship is very respectful but relaxed, as we have children in the same grade at school and we see each other at school functions and interact socially. They understand Paul's traveling situation, so MK allow me to be very flexible with my hours.

But it isn't all rainbows and lollypops. There is a downside to working for doctors. When MK start a conversation between the two of them using all their medical jargon know-how, I start to feel like a dumb-dumb. Now, I'm a college-educated woman with two degrees. I would call myself somewhat smart. But MK? They're **REALLY** smart. Mike is a Chiropractic Neurologist. As of this writing there are only about 350 in the world. On the weekends he teaches people how to be Chiropractic Neurologists. Kourtné is a Chiropractor who works with a lot of pregnant women, children and babies. Some mommies bring their constipated babies to Kourtné and watch out! It's a poop fest after she adjusts them. The babies are all happy afterwards. Who isn't after a good dumpy doodle?

Plus, Kourtné is one of those women who can juggle a million things and make it look effortless. She orchestrated buying a new building and moving their practice, including but not limited to creating the layout, decorating the new clinic and getting it all up and running. She recently put a new computer system into place at the office. She's on the board of this or that and volunteers at the soup kitchen, too. I'm exhausted just writing about it all. I'm not even going to mention she works out at 5 am. Truly, there is nothing this woman can't do. Oh, and by the way, she's also a mom of two children.

I, too, am a pretty independent woman who can be very busy (my nose may have just grown an inch), but I can't hold a candle to Kourtné. I tell myself that's okay because I pride myself on knowing how to relax. It really is a lost art. I know the weekends were meant for catching up on your sleep, watching movies and sporting events, maybe jumping on the elliptical while watching said movie or sporting event. Naturally, I have a To Do list, but if I get through the weekend with nothing crossed off I feel like I have accomplished something. I fist-pump the air and pat myself on the back knowing I have managed to avoid all manual labor and projects for another weekend. Unfortunately, no one I work with knows how to use their weekend as wisely as I do.

For this very reason I hate Monday staff meetings. Sometimes we go around the room and ask what everyone did over the weekend. Almost everyone is younger than me and they have a laundry list of things to share. Unfortunately, no one I work with understands the definition of the word "relax".

Jamie: "Dr. K, what did you do this weekend?"

Kourtné: "Thank you for asking. It was one of my most relaxing weekends in a while. I put in a new bathroom sink and faucet, tuck-pointed my fireplace and completed a slideshow for a family reunion. On Sunday I took my dog and we went on a twenty-mile hike. What did you do, Jamie?"

Jamie: "It *was* a relaxing weekend! I deep cleaned the apartment on Saturday and then John and I kayaked for eight hours. We also managed to train for our marathon. Oh, and he cooked me an amazing dinner of (insert here words about food that I have no idea what they mean and their official wine pairings). How about you, Dr. P?"

Mike: "I flew out to San Francisco and taught a class called Neuromuscular Applications. When I got back home Sunday night I had time to relax and build a fire pit in the backyard. What did you do, Carol?"

Me: "Um…just *relaxed*, like you guys." Insert major eye roll here.

When the new clinic was under remodel, Dr. K decided we could paint it ourselves (naturally) so I tried to pitch in whenever I could. One day I brought music and was playing it from my truck and I ran my battery dead.

Me: "Paul's in town. I'll give him a call and he can come jump me."

I called Paul but no answer so I leave a message, "Hey, Paul, come to the office and jump me. Tee hee." I'm so immature.

Kourtné: "Do you have jumper cables?"

Me: "What? Oh, I don't know. Let me check." I hunt around the back of my truck and open hidden compartments. "Hey, I found some!"

Kourtné: "Why don't you give them to me and read the instruction manual to make sure we're doing this right."

I hand her the cables and I am fumbling around for the manual. I am looking through the index on how to jump a car – Page 43. Now turning pages to page 43. I find it.

I look up from the book to tell her I found the right page. She already has both hoods up, cables attached and is waiting for me to start my truck.

Kourtné: "Just confirm what I did is right so we don't blow up."

Now, I know she is just doing this to humor me and make me feel like I was a part of her genius. Plus, she knows Paul is Mr. Safety and wants me to be able to tell him we referred to the manual.

Me: "Um...one red clip on my positive marker and one on yours. Then the black cable on your negative marker and the other attached to an unpainted metal surface that is not near the battery."

I turn the key. Car starts.

Me: "Wow! When was the last time you jumped a car? Please say yesterday."

Kourtné: "High school."

Me: "Well, of course it was."

Phone rings.

Me: "Hi Paul. No, you don't need to come over. Kourtné just jumped my car. Yes, I found my cables. Yes, we double-checked everything with the manual first to make sure it was right." I look at Kourtné and roll my eyes. "No, she doesn't moonlight at Jiffy Lube."

Paul on phone: "Damn. Kourtné is amazing. That's so hot."

Me sharing the conversation with Kourtné, "Paul 'Paris Hilton' Steingreaber says that is sooooo hot." She laughs and flips her hair.

Paul still going on and on about how he can't believe she knows how to jump a car. "Settle down there, cowboy. She still puts her pants on one leg at a time. I'm hanging up now."

Me: "Seriously, is there anything you can't do? I'm actually starting to get annoyed."

Kourtné: "I have a list of things I can't do and won't do. I tell Big Mike that if I ever start crossing stuff off *that* list he better be worried." Mike, consider yourself warned.

UNconventional Tip #30

Know When To Strangle Someone

Speaking of relaxing, I don't get to very often with my siblings and our families since we are spread out around the US of A, but every now and again the moon and stars align and we find ourselves together, usually in Iowa, to celebrate a special event, usually my parents' anniversary. This is an extremely rare occasion and incredibly important to me.

It was at one such gathering that Paul and I found ourselves hosting my siblings, their spouses and my parents for dinner one evening. I chose my favorite restaurant that was on a beautiful golf course. I had a private room reserved and everyone was dressed up. We started the evening sitting out on the patio having cocktails. Paul had committed to playing in a golf tournament that day, but *promised* me he would be at dinner on time. I was definitely concerned that Paul was going to blow this for me but he knew how important this dinner was. So as we waited for him to show up I tried not to think about all the times Paul had been late to special events because the golf course was backed up, play was slow, rain delay, frost delay, fog delay, too wet, lost balls, five-somes were allowed, carts were not allowed or the ninety-degree rule was enforced. If you haven't figured it out, Paul plays a lot of golf.

Now, my oldest sister, Theresa, who has been married three times but hit the jackpot with the third one, has some serious comedic chops. The first time she met Paul she said, "Carol, I really like Paul. He'll make you a great first husband." Everyone laughed (except Paul). She has continued this joke throughout the years.

So as we were sitting on the patio she leans over to me and whispers, "Look at the good-looking guy on the putting green. He looks a lot like Paul. Great second husband material." We are both laughing as I turn my head to look at the guy. No, it can't be. Impossible. My heart starts beating out of my chest. My ears are ringing and I can feel my face start to get bright red. I realize I am holding my breath and digging my fingernails into my clenched hands. Paul completely forgot about me, my family and the celebration. Triple play. My mother's words, "Marriage is not for wimps", blare in my head.

Theresa: "Well, damn if that isn't Paul! Not dressed for a formal dinner, but looking good in his golf shorts and baseball cap."

Theresa gets up from the table and walks over to the edge of the patio to get Paul's attention.

What is so frightening is that I know exactly what happened before Paul even got a chance to explain. That is what 27 years of marriage will do. He was playing in the tournament and was putting badly. He stopped by the local pro shop on his way home to test out a new putter he had his eye on, in the process completely forgetting where we were having dinner and that he was supposed to be showering and joining us.

Theresa's husband, Tom (a fellow golfer), looks over at me and assesses the situation immediately. He's a sharp one. Damn him. He knows exactly what has happened. He chimes in, "Well, well, well. I have to say there have been many times in my life that I wished I was Paul. When Paul hits his tee shot almost 300 yards I always say, 'I wish I was Paul'. When Paul gets a hole in one, I say, 'I wish I was Paul'. When Paul makes a thirty-foot putt to post a 68, I say, 'I wish I was Paul'. But, today, right now at this very moment, I am so very glad I am *not* Paul. Waitress, a round of drinks on me! I'm going to sit back and watch the show."

During Tom's soliloquy Theresa has gotten Paul's attention and he is walking up to the patio. The look on his face tells me he knows he is in deep doo doo. He's sweaty, grassy and his golf hat has dried sweat stains on it. But he does the smart thing and goes right over to my parents and congratulates them on their special day, and asks them if he should go home and change or can he join us wearing what he has on. Brilliant. Of course my parents don't give two licks what Paul is wearing and say, "Life's too short! Get a drink and pull up a chair!"

Well played, Paul. Well played.

After going around the group and greeting each of my family members individually, and everyone giving him a gentle ribbing about being late (no one even realized that he completely forgot, except Tom who was really, **_REALLY_** disappointed that I did not rip Paul a new one), Paul came over to me and whispered in my ear, "I really messed up. BIG TIME. You are so classy not make a scene on your parents' special night. That is just one of the many reasons why I love you. I will make this up to you. I promise."

Tom, watching very carefully my reaction to the words going into my ear and still hopeful there may be a scene, starts in. "Carol, what is Paul whispering in your ear? Paul, how did the tournament go today? You seemed REALLY surprised to see us. A little dazed and confused. Paul, did you get hit in the head with a golf ball? Do you have amnesia? Hi, I'm Tom."

That night, my sister Brenda actually saved Paul from being tackled on the putting green and the putter being wrapped around his neck. She was sitting next to me the entire time, with her hand under the table, squeezing my leg so hard that her nails were digging into my skin and my leg was going numb. There was no way she was going to let me out of that chair to ruin a rare evening of all of us together. The baby of the family always gets what she wants.

Well played, Brenda. Well played.

UNconventional Tip #31

Have a Pick-Me-Up File

I know I heard Mom say a hundred times, "Being a mother can be a thankless job." And "I can't have nothin' nice." The second comment always came after we broke her favorite coffee mug or got some nasty stain on the couch that wouldn't come out.

I get it. We have all been there. You've had an exhausting day and sit down for the first time at 9:30 at night to hear, "Mom, I have a huge project due tomorrow. Do we have any poster board?"

At my first out-of-college job, I kept a "Pick-Me-Up" file. If I had a great review or someone complimented me on my work, I would write down the words and put them in the file to pull out on a different day when someone was chewing my ass about something.

I did the same thing when I became a stay-at-home mom. I call it my "Surprise Box". Whenever the kids or Paul would do something special that really knocked me off my feet, it would go in my Surprise Box. Now, I am 49 years old and granted, the box has yet to be spilling out and overflowing, but it's great to have when I'm having a bad day or missing my kids.

The homemade cards kids make when they are little are priceless. The homemade cards that kids make when they are in college and can truly appreciate their parents after living away from home are keepsakes.

I had waited 20 years for these words. I knew they would come someday. Years of me shouting to her (as she stormed into her bedroom and slammed the door), "You'll thank me one day!" had finally set in. This was the moment I had waited for. This card went into my "Surprise Box" the moment after I read it. I was blessed to receive this card from Kate (she was a junior in college at the time) on Mother's Day.

Hey mom!

It's mother's day!

Flowers for my mom!

me, fresh out of placenta

#1 mom

foam finger

Mom,

Happy mother's day to my mom! I am so blessed to have a mom who is so funny, smart, loving, thoughtful, caring, strong, wise and many more (positive) adjectives. I hope I can be like the woman and mother you are when I have my own kids. You are truly amazing and so special to me. Thank you for teaching me how to clean the house and make eggs and how to laugh at yourself and not take everything so seriously. Thank you for teaching me to find happiness in the little moments life gives us. Thank you for teaching me to be independent but also to cherish my friendships. Thank you for supporting me in my schoolwork and in my life in general. Thank you for telling me that I am special. I love you so much mom!

love, Kate

Here's what the inside of the card said:

Mom,

Happy Mother's day to my mom! I am so blessed to have a mom who is so smart, loving, thoughtful, caring, strong, and wise and many more (positive) adjectives. I hope I can be like the woman and mother you are when I have my own kids. You are truly amazing and so special to me. Thank you for teaching me how to clean the house and make eggs and how to laugh at yourself and not take everything so seriously. Thank you for teaching me to find happiness in the little moments life gives us. Thank you for teaching me to be independent but also to cherish my friendships. Thank you for supporting me in my school work and in my life in general. Thank you for telling me that I am special. I love you so much mom!

Love, Kate

UNconventional Tip #32

Expect Accolades On Your Anniversary

Did I mention that Paul and I have been married 27 years? This didn't happen by accident. Lots of blood, sweat and wine went into this marriage. Every year on our anniversary I expect congratulations. From my children. My kids, Kate (a senior in college) and Nick (a sophomore in college), have definitely benefited from this union and I expect acknowledgement and accolades on our big day.

Last year on our anniversary we heard from our daughter. A card arrived BEFORE our special day. A phone call AND a text on the special day. She's my overachiever. She gets it. She knows who butters her bread and is too brilliant (gets it from Grandma Colleen) to mess up a good thing. She's my thinker.

Nick was MIA. All day.

Now most moms would just let this slide. Right? But surely you've learned by now I am not like most moms.

The text I sent to my son the day after our wedding anniversary went something like this:

Hey, Jim. Guess what happened 27 years ago yesterday? Your mom and dad met and fell in love and got married. Because we chose wisely (and didn't marry all of the other attractive, funny people who came into our lives) your skinny little ass was born. And because we chose to sacrifice and save money our entire lives (forsaking all new sports cars, speedboats and mansions) your skinny little ass is walking around a college campus surrounded by mountains. I think this special day deserves a shout out from you thanking us for choosing wisely. We will still be accepting congratulations today and tomorrow.

Hit send button.

One minute later.

Phone rings. It's Nick.

Bam! That's how it's done, my friends.

UNconventional Tip #33

Believe

I am going to share something with you that is very private. I mean *really* private. More private than breaking a glass table while making whoopee. More private than taking my pants off during my mammogram. More private than a story about me mooning my kids.

This is a story most people don't know. It is a beautiful gold nugget that I want to hold onto, to keep deep in my pocket. A story told to me by my precious Mother. A story I know she would demand

I put in this book if she were alive and sitting in her chair, drinking a Pepsi and smoking a cig. So, to honor my mom, I am sharing Sherri Ann's story. I saved it for the end because I didn't want to share it with just anyone. It had to be saved for my faithful readers who read my entire book and stayed with me on my unconventional road through life and motherhood. By the way, thank you for taking the time out of your busy life to read about mine.

The reason Mom and Dad always told us "Don't take life so seriously because tomorrow isn't promised" is because tomorrow wasn't promised to my sister, Sherri Ann. In 1964, at the tender age of five, she was diagnosed with leukemia. My parents were told she had six months to live if she went into a really good remission. But Jesus had other plans and gave us Sherri Ann until May of 1969. Remember my family picture in chapter two where Dad was holding Sherri Ann's hand? She was nine in the picture and it had been almost four years since her diagnosis. My parents lived their mantra "Don't take life so seriously because tomorrow isn't promised" every day for those five years, and every day after. They made those five years as special as they could for Sherri Ann. They reminded her and all of us that every morning we wake up is another day to enjoy. Well, do our chores first and then enjoy.

My parents, together with another couple who lost a child to cancer, started the very first St. Jude Children's Parent Support Group in Cedar Rapids, Iowa. My parents changed the lives of hundreds of families. At Mom's funeral many people said to me, "Colleen helped us through the most devastating time of our lives. We will never forget her." My mom, who was not the most empathetic woman in the world, who made fun of me before my colonoscopy, who wouldn't take my dad to the hospital and so on, listened to families in their darkest hour and helped them heal. The layers of my mother are mind-boggling.

But this chapter is Sherri Ann's story and must be told before I end my book. Why, you ask? Because most people are not fortunate enough to have a first-hand account that Jesus is the real deal.

It was May 24, 1969. Sherri Ann was resting in her bed. Mom always kept her door open so she could be by Sherri Ann's side the minute she woke up. Sherri yells for Mom to come close her door – an unusual request. Mom grants Sherri her privacy. About fifteen minutes go by, and then Mom hears Sherri call her name. She gets up out of her kitchen chair and goes to open Sherri's door.

Mom: "You okay?"

Sherri Ann: "Mom, am I going to die?"

Now, up to this point, no one had talked about death. It was always "Sherri's getting better" or "Sherri's in remission". I mean, come on, it was 1969 and she had already lived five years longer than the doctors had predicted. My family is very faith-filled and we always leave the door open for the Lord to work a miracle.

Mom: "Why are you asking me that?"

Sherri Ann: "Because somebody just visited me and said I was going to die but not to be scared. They said I was going to be with Jesus soon." Two days later my sister was in Jesus' loving arms.

Believe. As unconventional as it might seem in this day and age, just believe.

"Sharing The Love"

This book is dedicated to all the women in my life that make me laugh. You know who you are. Thank you for not taking yourselves so seriously, and enjoying life with me.

Paul, Kate and Nick, my inspiration. Thank you for all of your encouragement and support while I wrote my dream. You know how much I love and adore you.

My amazing father, Jerry, and all my siblings, Theresa, Rick, Sherri Ann (my Guardian Angel), Marty, David and Brenda, thanks for providing the material and the laughter. Keep it coming.

Paul's wonderful parents, Carol and Don, thank you for raising an incredible man and being such a blessing to us.

To the University of Iowa Children's Hospital and to St. Jude Children's Research Hospital, for all the work you are doing so that fewer and fewer children ask, "Am I going to die?"

Lastly, this book is a very special dedication to my mother. During my visit with her in her hospital room on Tuesday December 11, 2012, she was excited because the doctor was going to release her to go home the next day. She said, "I'm leaving this hospital tomorrow come hell or high water." She always had to be right and usually was. She went home to her Heavenly Father and her beloved daughter, Sherri Ann, on 12/12/12. Mom loved to play the slots. She pulled out all the stops and passed away on this day so we would know God has a sense of humor. Love and miss you, Mom. Thanks for always making me laugh.